# STEP GENERATION

# Step Generation

## An American Emplosion

David Ballard

Copyright © 2010 by David Ballard.

| | | |
|---|---|---|
| Library of Congress Control Number: | | 2010901910 |
| ISBN: | Hardcover | 978-1-4500-4211-6 |
| | Softcover | 978-1-4500-4210-9 |
| | E-book | 978-1-4500-4212-3 |

All rights reserved. No part of this book may be reproduced or transmitted in any form or by any means, electronic or mechanical, including photocopying, recording, or by any information storage and retrieval system, without permission in writing from the copyright owner.

This book was printed in the United States of America.

To order additional copies of this book, contact:
Xlibris Corporation
1-888-795-4274
www.Xlibris.com
Orders@Xlibris.com

72242

# SOME CHAPTERS

Intro ................................................................................................ 7

Understanding .................................................................................. 9
What Will I Receive? ........................................................................ 12
The Need for Someone to Step Up ................................................... 13
To Walk or not to Walk .................................................................... 15
Rescuerszz ....................................................................................... 17
To Go on A Drive ............................................................................ 19
Smother out following hate . . . ....................................................... 22
Mom and Dad Happily Ever After . . . ............................................ 24
An Inheritance ................................................................................ 25
CPR ................................................................................................. 27
Before You Step Up, You'd Better Get Ready For The Climb .......... 28
Clean the Mirror of Your Life. What Do You See? ........................... 30
A Moment to Embrace .................................................................... 36
But I'm all alone and it's the holiday's ............................................. 37
Assessment ...................................................................................... 40
Truly Alone ..................................................................................... 42
The Inner Circle .............................................................................. 46
Step One Would you like to dance? ................................................. 47
Public Intoxication Are You within the Limits? ............................... 50
Take Time to Focus ......................................................................... 51
Safeguards of Slowing Down ........................................................... 54
Respect for Self, Children, and the Ex ............................................. 56
Do you have All the Answers? ......................................................... 58

| | |
|---|---|
| Are you an ECM | 60 |
| Whose Turn Is It? | 62 |
| I Knew This Day Was Coming | 63 |
| Please Don't Step On My Toes | 65 |
| The Price For Admission | 66 |
| Youngsters Don't Think | 69 |
| Holidays Are a Hoot | 70 |
| Hammering Out the Holidays | 71 |
| Preparing For a Glamorous Garden | 76 |
| Don't Pass on the Pity | 79 |
| The Variety of Life | 81 |
| Picking Battles | 83 |
| Sounds Like a Fun Ride | 85 |
| Good Friend Vs Good Find | 87 |
| Love? | 90 |
| Coach's Perspective | 94 |
| Boys to Men | 96 |

# Intro

Basically, the enemy we face in our country today is not an enemy attacking from the outside of our border but an enemy embedded within. Freedom cannot thrive if the family unit does not survive. Without an understanding of noble sacrifice, serving others, or divine accountability, we are doomed. The time is critical. We need men to step up to the plate of leadership, we need women to come alongside, and we need abandonment to be abandoned.

As mentioned on the backside of this book, I am a product of this loose lifestyle myself, and as I matured into a young adult, I just fell into my place of hurting and misleading others too. This may be a similar lifestyle that you are in or came from. I did not truly understand the destruction that I was distributing until I looked at the wake I was leaving behind me in this lifestyle. So where did my personal change come from in my life? First of all, my personal change wasn't as easy as a oil change at Walmart. No it was more like an engine overhaul by NASCAR. Disassembly of thoughts and lifestyle is part of of the process. Reassembly with perseverance, grace, and love is must in order to foster a changed life. Between the self help books, shots of tequila, A.C.A. meetings, a couple sixpacks, some acid trips, divorce, counciling, and losing my car a couple times, plus a dozen or so girlfriends, I finally opened a book my grandmother had given me. This book introduced me to Jesus. Now please don't drop this book and run. I'm not here to convert or preach, but I wouldn't be honest if I didn't mention the Bible and Jesus. Through both I've learned the ability to love others as I would have liked to be loved as a child, sacrificial, unadulterated, and kind—love that leads to the building up of others, not only to build my family directly but mankind as a whole. People obviously learn how to love by the example given them by their parents. The model lived out before them is the foundation of which they'll build their lives on. Women won't reach their full potential as an adult until they have made the decisions required of a mother, and boys won't grow up and become men until they are challenged to serve their own family and not themselves.

**Even if you don't believe in the Bible as an inspired word of God, Jesus taught us to be accountable to something bigger than ourselves and to love our neighbor as ourselves. If we could just put those two things into action, "first" in our lives, then our families' lives. Our communities would thrive and not have to get into welfare lines, abortion lines, or battle lines . . .**

This book and workbook to follow are designed to give you, the reader, a better perspective of how challenging the step life can be. Whether you're the parent or the stepparent, the challenges and frustrations will be unique to your marriage. Sometimes you may feel like you're shipwrecked on an island all alone in the ocean of life, because when you speak to friends or family they don't have an ex to deal with. They don't have children to deal with children that aren't biologically theirs. They don't have the feelings of frustration when the other parents rules are mentioned in defiance or that parent does something that you disagree with and you have no control to change their influence. Anyway, these things and more will be dealt in later chapters, so read on, soldiers.

# Understanding

We must come to an understanding that all of the characters involved in this unification are usually wounded souls in search of relief. This is the first big step. A healing of wounds is needed more than a direction of life and right or wrong guidance. When attempting to balance your daily life, the application of "healing and forgiveness" more than rules and obedience is needed. If forgiveness isn't practiced, this blending of two families will be in constant turmoil. Actually, a more appropriate example is we have to give grace. Grace is forgiveness plus reward—not rewarding their actions which may not align with your expectations, but rewarding the relationship that you have an opportunity to help forge.

*Adjustments have to be made by all involved: dog, cat, kids, Mom, Dad, step on, Grandparents, fish, etc.*

First and foremost, when these families are unified, it must be understood that often each family has preestablished survival mechanisms and communication systems in place. In comparison, when we look at various interactions from our life experience, we may think that their reaction is weird and needs to be changed. But does the way that they do some things really need to be changed to our way? It's like going to the store to get some items, we can walk, ride a bike, drive a car, push a skate board, pull a cart, ride a bus, or even have the store deliver the items. Are any of these ways of obtaining items from the store wrong? No. But if your old like me you probably would prefer to drive over pushing a skate board or pulling a cart. Yet, the children you come in contact with may prefer to walk and pull a cart to the store. Now, because your the "adult", you can ascert your will and make them go in the car.

This is the first hint of a bad attitude and rough interactions to come in this relationship if you have to force things to go your way. Conflict has now been introduced over the simplest thing and only because it had to be done the way that you want to do it. Let them walk. You can still drive and meet them or better yet walk with them and get some exercise. Sometimes in life we need to live with not getting our way just because we can. And don't worry, you'll have plenty of opportunities to engage in conflict during this raising of children to young adults.

Using an example of an oak tree poem, here's what you may find if you look beyond the first impression and look deeper into the root of the tree or people involved.

There was once a great oak tree that wasn't as tall as all the rest.

And although it wasn't as tall it stated, "I have more wood I am the best". All the other trees just laughed and swayed in the wind. They told the smaller tree to stop and said "please do not pretend". Then came the day that the lumber jacks come and pick the trees to cut. They pointed here and pointed there, but at the smaller tree they stopped . . . . The surrounding trees could not contain themselves swaying in the wind, but then you could have heard a leave drop when the lumber jacks voice boomed in. Here's the tree we've been looking for of all the tales told past. You see this trees trunk had grown along the ridge it's wood a valued catch. With the nutrients and added roots it adapted to be much stronger. So the woods value was very high for making a table for someones grandmother.

The lesson here is for us not to base our expectations on first impressions or the words of others. You see we must understand that much like this tree story, everyone will bring a unique them into the situation at hand. All of us have a valued piece to place in the puzzle of life.

So, now you may be thinking, get to the point, lumber boy?

The point is that these adaptive traits of a tree coping and learning to survive are similar to the children and parent of a single-parent household, and, much like the adaptive tree, they'll have abilities that you'll not be able to see on the surface or at first glance, yet have to respect.

So, point-blank, some of the adaptations that this family has had to make, in order to function, will not be let go of by the child or the parent even if they truly want to. These adaptive traits have become part of their character as a family unit.

Yet, with some understanding and grace over and over again, you'll learn to cope in order to navigate through the storms of the "step life."

Remember this, as an adult coming into the situation, you "volunteered" to join, and the children didn't ask for your opinion.

**So until they do ask, you may be asked to simply . . . zip it!**

# What Will I Receive?

Often going into this situation, with all good intent, a step on parent will come in thinking, *if I marry into this family "I can" bring stability* . . . As a child, in this situation, the thinking is, "*If my parent found the love of . . . their life*" *all would be better and "I'd have" a family* . . . As a parent, those involved, think, *if I had some help "I'd have" joy back in my life.*

To some extent, these statements carry truth, but beyond the romanticism, the statements are quite self-serving and empty. The reason they are empty is because the statements are about personal gain not family unity.

In order to truly graft ourselves into something else, we have to cut parts of us away and meld into whatever it may be. **Sacrifice** . . .

**Two main points will often start or end each chapter of this book. These points are that the children's needs are first priority and the step on parent can leave if they can't hack it. God first, family second, lover . . . last. This applies to both parents' priority for the family. Once you make it, don't break it!**

# The Need for Someone to Step Up

So why would a Mother have children just to abandon those children for career, beer, or sexual cheer? Why would a Father have children just to allow another man the opportunity to embrace and raise his children? Also, why would people, who are so attracted to each other that they have three children together, decide that they need to dissolve the security of their family in order to find sanity?

*Now*, more importantly though, why would a perfectly sane adult, also known as a step on parent, even sign up to raise someone else's toddler, teen, or turnstile, twenty-something single-parent child?

So let's first take a peek at what you're in store for when you start your step-generation journey in life. Here's some of what's to be expected for your exciting life of sacrifice, stepping up, and stepping into someone else's existence.

Before you step up, you'd better get ready to get stepped on.

Before you step up, you'd better get ready for the climb.

Before you step up, you'd better get ready to get sucker punched.

Before you step up, you'd better get ready to be with the family, yet you'll feel alone.

Before you step up, you'd better get ready for the finances to go crazy. Then, be asked to buy toothpaste, tampons, and tennis shoes.

Simply stated, you better be ready to not be ready . . .

Does this sound rewarding, profitable, or fun? Fantasy is fun. Profit is for Wall Street. Rewards are few and far between. Remember, family is whatever you're willing to sacrifice for it. It's not to say that there won't be moments of happiness, accomplishment, and unity, but reality says get ready for a unique opportunity to grow.

# To Walk or not to Walk

Now, if you're still here reading or you're already a step on parent, my praises go out to you. If you're a person who after reading the aforementioned is questioning, what the heck am I getting myself into? Should I stay and play or should I tie my shoes, retreat, and get stepping? I say find the door, give your thanks, and get trucking if you have, "any", question of your commitment. The reason for this is because we as adults do our dance of destruction, which is rooted in our needs (sexual, financial, social), and our children take the emotional hit. Then as a way to cope with our self-serving stupidity, the children learn to shut down love as a way to not feel the pain of abandonment, again, again, again . . . Shame on us.

Now, as an adult volunteering for this vastly dynamic situation, you have no idea of the scope of enteral and external emotional conflict you'll be asked to endure. Also, the amount of heartache and confusion you'll be inflicting on the children by promises and hope destroyed if you take on this monumental task without commitment to stay committed.

In other words, what is your purpose for this marriage? Just like having your own children you must be able to set most of "your" sex, finances, and social events on hold from zero to eighteen years minimum.

(This is the time, *right now, as adults, to sit and discuss the function of this family unit*, define the task at hand). I have written a workbook just for this purpose. One major question is, is this going to be a "Raise the children and move on with your lives," or is this going to be a "Raise the children and turnstile them and their family constantly back into your home?" Many stepparents get caught and are miserable because family is family, and the alone date time, up all night, crazy sex gets minimized once the family becomes priority.

This is fixable through your attitude becoming flexible. Focus has to be shifted to their need. It's just that once you've joined the family, family will wear you down unlike anything else, especially if you have not raised a family before, and, might I add, if you're raising the family properly. Attitude adjustment is essential.

Now you may ask, what is proper? A simple answer for what is an assessment of what is right is: If each child or children is immersed into something that is a healthy challenge, they truly enjoy. The things that the "children" enjoy could be anything from singing to playing instruments, to playing sports, to acting in drama, to reading books, to about anything their imagination and your pocketbook can afford. If they simply don't seem to be attracted to anything mentioned, then you may want to investigate all of the various martial arts systems. A good way to do this at one time is to attend an open international tournament. I recommend the San Diego Grand Internationals.

Love you, Mr. G. So, as you can see, the money and energy has to be shifted.

I'ts not, Oh I'm married now so we can't do this or that anymore, because we got the children, no it has to be here we go as a team to take on this opportunity to impact our lives and our childrens lives in a positive way. So, "I" must be set aside so my family can thrive. Once, married we're not dating so much anymore, but focusing on the childrens needs they have to be job one and valued through action, time, and love. Our task at hand is to raise our children into full functioning adults, but better than that we can give them the opportunites we may not have had. This could be monitary, emotionally, stability or any combination thereof.

Once again, with our attitude we either bring altitude into the relationships or darkness which can engulf all that is good. That leads us into our next chapter.

# Rescuerszz

Although it may be hard to imagine these children, who seem to view us as a knight in shining armor or a princess of promise, to cause us any major headache or heartache, inevitably they will. It's just simple adult/child interaction. Sooner or later, while interacting with them, there will come the moment of no. The reason why we say no doesn't matter because they are children in need of leadership, not friendship. Also, we are all human and have our limitations intermixed with our moments of frustration. Remember, all knights in shining armor . . . burp and have times that the armor gets tarnished, and all of the princesses of promise . . . fart and wake up without makeup. Yikes!

In this sometimes-crazy lifestyle, there has to be an understanding of the action of sacrifice. The picture that resonates this action of sacrifice most in my mind is from the movie, *Passion of the Christ*. Jesus, the main character of the movie, has been beaten, betrayed, and belittled. As the blood that is left in his body still flows from wounds undeserved, he crawls toward his destiny and purpose in life. The purpose for his life was to be sacrificed for the benefit of all humanity on earth, and he willingly crawled and laid himself on the cross. Now even he inquired from God for another way to accomplish this task, but when no other way was acknowledged, he accepted his duty, which ***he had volunteered*** for. Remember, in the situation you're climbing into, that ***the children didn't ask for your help*** as a parent or a step on parent you volunteered your support, finances, and life for at least eighteen years. Rent the movie ***passion*** if you can.

For Christians, this movie is a well-done example of self-sacrifice and suffering for others and the ultimate act of devotion from God toward his creation.

As parents, we have to look to our children's lives as an opportunity to give, not to get. The rewards along the way are, well, worth all the sacrifice that is needed, but remember once again, rewards of raising responsible, functioning children are usually not immediately satisfying and require uncompromising commitment.

The more disruption you're willing to endure for their sake, the better the chances are that they will be successful in life.

Consequently, in the beginning of this book, I started by praising one person who's being stepped on and warning another person to step "way" around and step "way" clear of the situation before them if they cannot commit for more than two to three minutes at a time.

The aforementioned was written as an opportunity to take a pause and open your mind for a moment before you take on this momentous task, and also to hopefully, help all the folks responsible for this union to be made more aware of some of what's to be expected as you venture into **"the step zone**."

Being real is not an option, it's mandatory. Now, let's take a drive.

# To Go on a Drive

I understand the great pull that we all experience on some level to be a part of a family unit. Some say that the drive for a family is an unquenchable drive that borderlines a divine inspiration from within us all. We see this drive taking place from preschool to elementary school, to high school, and to the school of hard knocks. It seems that we are all driven to unite and fight.

The problem with in this war zone, also known as the step life, is that, this war will have most of its battles fought within our own mind, body, and spirit.

Also, since the evolutional educators of today think that we are not much more than some molecules set in motion by a lightning bolt that just appeared from nothing, and that the thought of a divine anything would be stupid, we'll title that drive as a basic survival instinct. How we acquired this mechanism isn't as important as attempting to have an understanding of it.

This basic instinct is a self-serving something or other that has us all looking out for numero uno, number one, the big me. Are you feeling me? . . .

The people interacting in this situation may have all good intention to help while in the fog of fantasy, and they'd even be willing to sacrifice all they have for love. Yet through the process of being stepped on, the romanticism "they" envisioned doesn't come to fruition. We start to departmentalize the relationship and blame the children for being children, demanding, unthankful, and uneducated on life. We start to view them as the problem and not as a tool of reflection to how we really are. As stated earlier many go into relationships in a self serving attitude and not as a servant to the situation. Then, after some time, we feel like a third person on a two-person date and ultimately start interacting with the family through bitterness and resentfulness.

Therefore, we the people (the stepparent, knight in shining armor, or princess of promise) become more of a liability and a perpetrator of social dysfunction in the overall situation than if we just steered clear of this tempting situation and didn't allow the stepfamily mark of madness to manifest its self in all of the lives involved. Whew! That was a mouthful.

Listen, most of us know someone who is doing the stepfamily lifestyle, and most are struggling in one way or another. They need encouragement and a dose of fact that raising children in general has its moments of frustration to say the least. True? True.

Truthfully though, in this step on situation, are there moments of bliss? Yes. Are there moments of accomplishment? Yes. Are there moments that this situation actually does have a semblance of a family unit? Yes.

But we must remember that these moments are just that . . . moments, and moments will pass. Enjoy them, employ them, and eventually, they will become more and more of a part of everyday life. We just have to stay rooted in Newton's law, and Newton basically states what goes up must come down. Now, only with time, each time we come down from our high, the landing should be less of a crash and more of a transition from euphoria back to reality. Life in Stepville can function in a very high and civil manner.

Even in an actual family, past, and reality set in. Newborns require enormous amounts of attention. Children the same amount just a different funneling of energy. Now of course, teens will be teens. Whether biological or not, they are usually difficult somehow, and I describe them simply as self-serving hormones of humanity.

In-laws are just that—those in the family who try to institute "their laws" into your family. In fact, because of some of the damage they impart, they should be classified as *outlaws*.

Basically, the jest of all this is that, to the children, even though you may be really cool, the parent that they are missing is the source of cool, and deep down, a big part of them would really like to see some sort of reconciliation. Get my drift? Biting my hook? Banging my gong?

# Smother out Following Hate . . .

Smothering out hate begins by not engaging in the whole this household against their household.

It's a natural response for us as people to show allegiance toward those who we are more closer in proximity to. One common way that this allegiance is usually shown is by word *bashing* or *acting* out toward the ex-friend, lover, acquaintance, wife, or husband. To engage in this bantering is a two-edged sword. Even if statements are true to an extent, maturity has to reign here.

First, there are two sides to every story. Second, if it's an ex-wife or ex-husband that you have made fun of or talked down about, it truly shows your intelligence in picking them and all the cut downs are a real reflection of the person you chose to make children with. Realize that at the most eighteen years of thorough interacting has to take place with this other parent in a civil manner. The courts demand it. Third, children are children and whatever serves them best in your presence, they also search for while in the presence of the other parent . . .

I've found that the children will do this bashing type of communication in an attempt to show a shift in allegiance. What a horrible life to be thrust into. Basically, most often their allegiance lies with whatever serves them best at the moment, as does most of our motives, and teens will especially take this to a new level.

Plainly, as flattering as it may seem to be exalted, this is a balloon ready to burst once the opportunity arises. In our society, which has its comedy deeply rooted in sarcasms, it's easy to take potshots and play the other parental figure as a fool. Just remember, "Those which hurt us the worst are those we love the most." Downplay this flattery of being on a pedestal and teach respect of adults and authority, then move on.

# Mom and Dad Happily Ever After . . .

We, the step on parent, second or fifth husband or wife, have to accept that on some level we'll always be number two in the children's hearts.

And if you team up with the part of them that wants to solidify their shredded life, you'll usually be much more accepted. You'll be viewed as a hero if you truly help them sift through their shattered life, *and not just remind them how messed it is*. Once again it cannot be reiterated enough do not put down, belittle, or bash the ex-lover, ex-husband, ex-wife or ex-step, is to make your own authority in the house belittled. Even if the whole family that you're joining is doing this destructive deed, do not participate. This bantering is like an infection of cancer that can grow undetected until it's too late to deal with or to deal with it is a massive surgical procedure. Nobody wins. The parent that you've partnered with loses respect due to dumb decisions. You lose respect due to the fact that you chose them also. The children on some level get angry because it is their mom or dad that's being disrespected, and finally but more importantly, you're teaching your children to disrespect adult authority. These children are just tattered souls of adult stupidity, and they didn't sign up for this existence.

Do you realize that there are family lives where children are happy to see their parents and eat breakfast together each morning? Do you realize that there are homes without knock-down, drag-out fights every weekend in the presence of children, God, and the neighbors? Is this the atmosphere that you want to foster for your children to grow up in. Would you have enjoyed that childhood? Or maybe you did grow up this way, . . . now you have a chance to change that. Change the inheritance of your grandchild by changing your today.

# An Inheritance

Bottom line is in becoming a step on parent you'll inherit all the parental responsibility with little or no accolades. So why would anyone do such a thing to themselves? I'll ask you again? Why are you about to step into this world of belonging, knowing that you really don't belong? Well, that statement isn't totally fair. It's not that you or I don't belong, it's just that we have to be able to accept where we do belong or more importantly how we can contribute to the team that we now belong to.

As an adult joining the family, it is not about telling people what to do but showing them how to do it. Although, the most frustrating thing is realizing, after showing them five hundred and three times how to do something, they simply don't, won't, or want to do "*it!*" Even if doing the said task, makes more sense the way you're showing them. Some of it could be rebellion, could be they're just set in their way, or could be, simply that either way is fine. We, as the joining piece to this scattered puzzle, can't take this opposition personally.

It's like inserting a square into a circled hole. This cannot be done unless the square is trimmed, cut, or modified to fit. Or the circle has to have the ability to flex, expand, and adjust in order to engulf the square. Remember, patience and truth will win out even after you've pulled all your hair out. Often we just need to be real with our reasoning and figure out if a situation is really worth going to war over. More importantly though is realizing that just because you can win the battle it doesn't mean you were necessarily right, and over all you'll not win the war as constant conflict will be the staple of the household.

## Enjoying your walk so far? OK

You'll observe, as you read this journey of stepping here and stepping there, that more than anything else you better watch where you step. Getting ready for this life is no walk in the park, and the footprints you leave behind will have an everlasting effect on the children that you've come in contact with.

We, too often, only look at the gain we enjoy in a moment instead of the long-term effect we have enacted. We will pollute the oceans and lakes when we're on vacation to fish and to be entertained.(Don't get me wrong), I'd fire up my two-stroke outboard for an opportunity to bag a bass in a heart beat, but at what cost in the long run will I affect those around me? Here lies the quandary of the step on lifestyle.

We, as adults, have to put our own wounded lives aside, and as adults, really focus on the children being valued over the adults involved. Then present a life as you both would have liked to have experienced it.

Sadly, divorce doesn't teach our children to not do divorce but quite the opposite it teaches it as an option. Once a parent divorces, the likelihood of their children divorcing is 50 percent higher than children who have grown up in an intact family. That number increases for each generational episode of divorce in the parent's family. The national average of divorce is 50 percent. So if your parents divorced and now you have divorced, the chance of your children staying in an intact family is now 75 percent less likely. In other words, there is a 75 percent chance that they will have to suffer similar pain and worse, the potential children, your grandchildren, will suffer the same life that you've just experienced. So how do we pump life back into this tradgedy? It's as easy as A,B,C. Set adolescence aside, Be the parent you would have liked to be, commit, commit, commit

# CPR

As a grown-up, whose choices have placed you into a place of responsibility to the children involved, you must look to the CPR "Code of commitment". It's as easy as ABC. First, be sure that your not being an obstruction for the Air flow of life into or out of the family. Secondly, be sure that the air flow that you put into the family Breathes life into it's existence and fosters hope. Lastly, there has to be circulation nutrients of love, direction, and peace in the home.

Also, and this is paraphrased. Once you start CPR, you're responsible to maintain care until life is restored or the victim is declared dead by a professional. Are you that committed to the family?

Simply, CPR isn't about your life, it's about theirs. All the emotional and physical abilities you have to foster life must be expended before you quit. Once again once you start CPR it's not about you any longer. Ka-beesch?

# Before You Step Up, You'd Better Get Ready For The Climb

The unification of this situation is like climbing a mountain. All your training, nutrition, and hydration can be defeated by simply not being outfitted properly. (Get books on various ages of the children you'll be engaged with.)

The gear has to be able to withstand a great amount of stress for a great amount of time.

Preparation, preparation, preparation—the only thing you can be sure of is, where you lack is where you'll be attacked. That rhymes, huh? Even if you have or have had children, this situation will have its own personal experiences, some similarities for sure, but there are different personalities involved which will evolve differently. Wherever you're stepping into the situation, it's already experienced a life of ***its own***. This mess already has its own survival mechanisms B.Y. (before you).

It comes down to visualization. We have to prepare for the worst and see the best in order to sustain a winning attitude. Where a general goes so, too, does his army. In order to function like a unit, you have to live like a unit. Make good times happen. Foster good memories through adventures in life. Take the family to the park, to the beach, to the mountains, to the river, to the mission field, and most importantly, to the Grandma and Grandpa's home.

The Grandparents allow for some parental R and R, and the children get away with some things that they're not supposed to do around Mom and Dad.

Also, time with Grandma and Grandpa allows a connection to the roots of the past identity.

So what examples of lifes adventures and what to do and what not to do are you teaching your children?

When children are in the comfort zone of their homes they can function pretty self sufficiently. I mean with the microwave, TV, and video games what more does a child need. Well, a good camping trip in the mountains can allow them to experience life outside these urban boxes called home. Climb a tree, try to catch a fish or simply attempt to hike to the hill that is right over there, gives a new perspective to life and it's elements. For a little more appreciation take them on a weekend that it is supposed to rain. Talk about taking on a mountain. Be sure to pack the coffe and coaco.

# Clean the Mirror of Your Life. What Do You See?

(It's time to feel the pain. Put the mouthpiece in and the groin protection on ... fight!)

Realities check for Mom or Dad. At this point, in your children's life, how many boyfriends or girlfriends have your children had to endure? What are you teaching them about commitment? Furthermore, do not attempt to pass the blame onto your ex-loser and what they may have taught the children when it comes to disciplining them. They must be taught to respect elders. Remember, in actuality, all *that* you can affect is whatever you are teaching them while in your home.

What strategies to cope with life are you teaching them? Are you teaching them that whoever has the most excuses wins? Are you teaching them that life is not controllable, so we should just gamble with it until something good comes along? Are you teaching them the theme-park illustration of "Life is a roller-coaster drama of highs and lows, where life is lived by let's fight, let's make up, let's fight, let's make up, let's fight, let's make up? Or, do you teach strangulation safety? Safety only comes when we allow people one opportunity to screw up, then it's over. The old you cut me, now I'll cut you. Or, was it me, I cut you, now you can cut me or my favorite was, you can love me until I'm uncomfortable then you have to leave.

If you haven't done any of this merry-go-round of up-and-down, pony-parade lifestyle in front of your children, then my hat goes off to you.

Lord knows, that if I would have been the parent in charge of children after this world's psychological views, I'm sure I would have dealt some real damage to their interpretation of life. I myself am guilty of a ride or two. Especially since I used to buy into the teaching of, "These children are just little people, grown-ups in a small body, capable of making logical choices."

I'll agree that if you take a moment and explain a situation and let them choose, they can do that sometimes. But left to their own devices, unless the situation serves them in a personal gain of the moment, they usually won't do what's correct or safe. That responsibility and job is ours as adults in their life. As an adult, we see the future benefit or disaster. As a child, they don't see anything except food when they're hungry, playing with their friends, and a place to sleep when they're tired. Oh, how I long to return to a time when life was such as this!

So before you decide to move Mr. or Mrs. Right now in as a parental playhouse puppet, you better think twice; no, you better go on trip to the Bahamas with your friends and reflect on the beach. Drink too much, have annoying conversations of truth with yourself, wake up with a hangover, puke, and ponder. Or, if you're a Christian, seek pastoral council, pray for wisdom, and seek God's peace.

Simply, as a nation, we've lost what being a family teaches, like how to share, how to tolerate, how to love, how to be loved, how to be joyful for someone else, how to be kind, how to teach, how to be taught (seven-year-olds can do wonders), how to clean, how or when to be messy, how to think of others, how to have security, how to kill a gold fish, how to cuddle a puppy, how to feed a dog, how to wash a car, how to change a car spark plug, how to mow a lawn, how to paint a home, how to clean a window, how to mop a bathroom, and most of all, all of the reasons why we do what we do in our home in this thing called "**family**."

- Now, half of the children of our nation think logically and they adapt. At Dad's house I do this, and Mom's house this; the reason why she does that is because Grandpa said this to Grandma, and Dad's new girlfriend doesn't approve, and mom's new stud doesn't agree, and the dogs bark too much, blah, blah. What the heck? Shoot me. Here's some information that you can hang your thoughts on. Both children and

adults from broken families have higher rates of clinical depression. *Family disruption and low socioeconomic status in early childhood increase the long-term risk for major depression.[10]*
- seek formal psychiatric care at higher rates. Studies vary, suggesting from 5 to 21 times the risk, and vary over whether men or women are more seriously affected.*[11][12]*
- in the case of men, are more likely to commit suicide at some point in their lives, according to a study by Augustine Kposowa, a University of California at Riverside sociologist.*[13]*

This study quantified earlier work that estimated an increased risk of 2.7 times for men.*[14]* (cited in*[15]*)

- have lower life expectancies overall.*[16][17][18][19][20][21]*

Studies have also claimed positive correlations between divorce and rates of:

- *stroke[22]*
- *cancer.* Married cancer patients are also more likely to recover than divorced ones.*[23]*
- acute infectious diseases, parasitic diseases, *respiratory* illnesses, digestive illnesses, and severe injuries. See the article *Black Men And Divorce: Implications For Culturally Competent Practice.[24]*

In support of these particular claims, that article cites the U.S. Bureau of the Census Population profile of the United States in 1991*[17]* and an article by S. L. Albrecht on *Reactions and adjustments to divorce.[25]*

- heart problems. Some research suggests that childhood trauma, including parental divorce, can lead to much greater risk of heart attack in later life.*[26]*

Combined with job stress, divorce led to a 69% increase of death rate among men with above average risk of heart disease. *[27] Cites as source[28]*

- *rheumatoid arthritis* and *osteoarthritis*. A 2002 article in the Journal of Rheumatology shows a 30% increase in risk at any given age.*[29]* A 2003 article in the Canadian Journal of Public Health finds that parental divorce leads to increased risk of arthritis for children later in life.*[30]*
- *sexually transmitted diseases*. For example, in Uganda "Results from a baseline survey of HIV-1 infection in the cohort of over 4,000 adults (over 12 years old) showed a twofold increase in risk of infection in divorced or separated persons when compared with those who are married."*[31]*

The point of the aforementioned information is to understand the devastation that can take place as we as adults move from this relationship to that relationship. There will be a negative affect on your children that you will be directly responsible for. These articles can be investigated on Wikipedia free encyclopedia.

So how do we narrow the gap of destruction in our childrens lives? One way is to separate adult conversations to adult times. An example is arguments, agruments have to have there own place and time. The reason for this is because of the pressures and distractions that stepkids have to endure. When it comes to adult conflicts these conflicts should be resolved outside of the childrens ear shot. Their reactions to the fears of rejection and family dissolving is magnified in their minds. They have already lost unity once. Some conflicts are not concealable, but do the best you can to keep adult conversations in the adult arena. As the children go through their lives and especially adolescence, there can be anger and sadness, that may be constant each day, this has to be dealt with through grace and possibly with some family counciling. Our job is to have understanding even if we ourselves don't truly understand.

As our children share in our lives, they don't really have a choice on what they suffer through in the decisions made by the adults in their lives who are supposed to be sworn to protect them.

The negative lessons that our parents taught us don't have to continue to survive on the shattered dreams of our children.

The anger and confusion that we lived in, while growing up, needs to be replaced with greed and persistence.

**Greed,** we have to fight for our children to have a place to call home, and **persistence,** we have to fight and even die to ourselves in order to have that dream come to fruition. Whatever our parents were to us, as children it does not have to be relevant to the life we choose to live today. They are not responsible any longer. Their opinions are just that, opinions, once we jump into our own lives. Our life is now our picture to draw and share with our families' world. Simply going for a walk around the block and talking to your child will surprise you at what you may learn about your kid.

**So playing house is not an acceptable lifestyle,** for the girls anyhow . . . **sorry girls,** but the guys get to continue in this lifestyle. We're just guys and that's how we roll. I mean, if you're dealing out the cookie, I'm Chewbacca the Wookie . . . *whoa*!!! OK, OK, the guys have to stop being cookie monsters with no care as to where the crumbs fall. So, guys, your daughters and your grandchildren's lives depend on . . . it . . . *well* . . . **not doing** . . . it . . . I mean.

So spend some time in introspection and be honest with yourself. If you recognize some of this craziness in your life, it is caused by your current decision-making process, and if you do have some of these short comings, own the stupidity of those decisions to your children. This will help to reestablish some respect and allow sincere change to be introduced. You know what I mean, jelly bean? Sorry. Like my uncle used to say, "It's better to tint the windows in the car before summer arrives."

Because the day is coming when all your relationship research will be addressed, and your son or daughter will recall to you the lifestyle you lived before them, in front of them, and with them in tow; remember, they are living your life with you each day.

# A Moment to Embrace

### (Is your high—attitude training paying off?)

So how do you start this? Take a moment to embrace the children and let them now that they are the most important thing in your life, and together with them you'll teach them all you know so that they will be all their potential allows them to be and then some.

Details of our mistakes don't need attention so much as owning them and claiming responsibility. Now don't expect angels to sing and for the sky to part because of your newly found revelation. Most likely, their response will be rolling eyes and at least one deep sigh.

Oh, so you have a teenager too, and things look pretty bleak. Well, the reality to this point in life has been a hard road, but at least you gain some respect by showing honesty and instituting some changes. Now, will the children or the family buy this newly changed reality committed by you? I don't know. Ask yourself, "What would I think if I just heard me again for the hundredth time?" In order to gain allegiance, you'll have to stop clanging the cymbal of attention and start being doing and living. (Christian or not, grab a Bible, go to the glossary, and then go and read the book of James it's only five chapters. Since you have the book open, go to 1 John five chapters). These books will teach you basic life skills and bathe it in love.

# But I'm all alone and it's the holiday's

Being alone, it sounds so lonely . . . reality check, please! Do you realize that most of us bring seclusion in our lives through our own choices? Brought on by years of not listening to family, friends, counselors, or the Bible. By not embracing clear direction given by those who have everything to lose and nothing to gain by whether or not we adjust our lives. It's definitely not hard to be swayed from even our own consciousness, as we are bombarded daily with the lie that fulfillment has to be attained by externalism. Externalism being fast cars, hard abs, big . . . house, nice yard, elite job, elevated status, new home, hot guy hot chick, etc., so basically, our needs are placed at the forefront of our minds constantly. Do you realize that holidays were designed around giving . . . . either the sacrifice of the Fourth of July for the founding of this nation, or the thanks at each Thanksgiving Day through our history, (there are many), or ultimately, the giving of God's son, the Christ, Jesus for the reestablishment of a relationship with our creator. Each day we have an opportunity to give thanks for our breath today to help change someone else's life tomorrow. To be given an opportunity to sacrifice our wants for someone else's needs.

Optimally, as parents, our only focus, once we have children, has to be their development. For us to go a few holidays a year without a so-called significant other to fulfill our empty feeling and sexual stimulate us, is but a small price to pay for the healthy development of our children. Our children didn't pick us to raise and love them. We . . . made . . . their . . . existence . . . possible! If you complain about their performance in life, look at your own. The most awesome moment in you and your children's life is when you realize that you can make their life different than yours was. What a holiday present this could be. Oh, it may cost you twenty four hours of time each day, but they are well worth it. Reflection of our chaos can cause a catastrophic shift of our reality to a defining moment of triumph in their reality. Actually, holidays can be changed to be viewed as another day we have to grow, give, get, and guarantee a different outcome in our children's lives.

Besides, if you're a single parent and you do it right, you'll never really be alone. If you have three children in the house and you get active in their lives, between all the events and activities to participate in, you'll be going and going and going much of your free time. Now, you may have "feelings" of loneliness at times, but you'll never truly be alone. Simply when we get into the "Waa, waa I'm alone" mode, all that we usually want is sex. Just take a moment to reflect. For me, most of my dumbest moments happened when I was too alone and unwilling to tame the tiger, . . . wow! I'll continue in a moment, . . . honey! Sorry for the interruption, my wife and I needed to talk about something.

Where were we? Oh, ya, the tiger or tigress. I understand the need for adult conversation and all, but if it is in regard to the opposite sex, hormones, tequila, and waa, not a good mix. If you need to talk to someone, talk to the same sex, simplify your interactions of life, similar problems, and similar solutions. Hey, we all struggle with doing what's right and loneliness. Call someone who will lift you up when you're down, not take you to an alley and give you a shove into seduction.

Besides, there are only one or two holidays a year that showing up at the parents' house without a significant other in tow seems a bit awkward. Those holidays, of course, are Thanksgiving Day and Christmas, of which you can remind the parents about how thankful they were when terrible twelve-pack Terry didn't show for Thanksgiving Day last year. For Terry, a day off work without alcohol . . . inconceivable. Now Christmas, without a significant other, is simply . . . sad . . . No, actually, once we get our focus where it should be, thankfulness and hope, you'll realize that we are responsible to give our family first priority and that the powers that have such a constant influence on us, which are basically, anti-family, want us to do nothing more than whine about ourselves as your children once again lose you, . . . to you.

More often than not when we hook up with a significant other, it really is being done to fill a void in us and vice versa for them. If it's a healthy union, until you're married, prioritize holidays for family. Parties and after-work get-togethers are for friends. Family has to be number one in our lives, made sacred, and honored. To just haphazardly show up to family events with someone, whom we barely know ourselves, continues bad judgment and may put some of our relatives in unknown danger.

Now, if there has been a couple years of a committed relationship to Mr. and Mrs. Right now, they have already been exposed to Mom or Dad a couple times, and there is commitment and a ring, OK., bring them to a Christmas family function, but if you don't have at least some of the aforementioned, you're playing the holiday-house game which cost money, emotion, and usually ends up ugly in time.

So bottom line is how well do you know these individuals that you are exposing your family to?

So remember, we're only alone on the holidays if we separate ourselves from those who truly love us. Not those who have sex with us, stating that they love us.

# Assessment

### a day to remember

Have you ever taken time to assess where you acquired your standards for living life from? No excuse intended for my stupid actions in life, but my influences were: a self-serving Mom; a womanizing Dad; a heroin-addicted/ex-con stepfather; a couple heroin-addicted aunts and uncles; and a functioning alcoholic family that embraced me as their own. I was adopted at two, lost a sister, a dog, a house, Mom's spouse, and once again, security at age five. Listen, I can go on and on, but the reality is the hope I found in Christ for me, that my brother is now saved, my mom is now saved, my wife is now saved (her children know Christ and will have to decide someday), and that the current wake of my life being dispensed from the boat of my life is the gifts I bring into our lives through the power of Jesus Christ. I choose not to be a product of the sledge of which I was born. Did I swim in it for a while? Sure. But am I going to subject the children, placed into my care to it, hell no!!! hell? No! Am I saying for you to become a Christian? It can't hurt, but more so, we all must get a standard to live by. Unless we want to stay in stupidity, which the definition is repeated acts expecting different results, we must alter the coarse. I found Christ. You can follow your grandma or grandpa or a teacher, whatever you choose to embrace. But, character, integrity, and putting those intrusted to your care first has to reign supreme.

The stress level reduces as you focus on your children that you now get to decide the fate of—where, what, when, who, and how your family gets to go through the life. Once your children are eighteen, if their edge hasn't dissipated and you have totally abandoned your destructive life for them and yourself (as should be), show them the door. Hand them their freedom. Give 'em time enough to grab clothes, grab their shoes, and get the door . . . Later, Love you and see you at your birthday, Thanksgiving Day, and Christmas! This is very hard to do . . . emotionally. Whatever you do, do not threaten them with kicking them out of the house. If you say it, play it out. If not, then a threat, is a threat, is a threat. It's about as good as a pan of water on the stove, with out heat it just sits there and evaporates at its own pace. Now, if the young adult in your care is not doing drugs or breaking house rules, you can make their transition into adulthood quite pleasurable and loving. Teaching them to save for their apartment, furniture, dishes, etc. can be quite an eye opener Sadly and hopefully you don't have a life as I did and have them leaving home at fifteen as was my case. I myself wasn't such a bad Kid, but all the caos surrounding my daily life made me a sad individual in search of relief. I didn't go to drugs or alcohol as was lived out before me, I just abandoned my life with my mom and step dad. You don't want your children wanting to leave do you? This scar can take years to heal and being a scar it never truly goes away. It took me years before I truly embraced my mom again. Now if the child is disruptive and out of control with drinking, drugs, anger or alcohol . . . two ways to deal with it. Patients and phone call to the police at eighteen or military school if still under age. Take a loan out if you need to. It's better than the court taking your money and you may truly save their life. (male or female doesn't matter) Sometimes as adults we've allowed our children to become too damaged for our ability to cope or they simply have a rebellious spirit. The point is no more games are to played. One side note though, having to send your child away so a stud or studdette can move into your bedroom is not acceptable.

So, if they are of age and choosing to live in a dangerous lifestyle, you can simply do as a famous or some infamous talk show host states, "Here is the pink slip to your life." Don't let the door hit your backside on the way out. By the way, my car stays here, my cat stays here, my bed stays here, the armwa stays here, my extra cell phone stays here, my x box stays here, and whatever else your dad wants when he gets home, stays here. OK, you can have your toothbrush and underwear. See ya!

# Truly Alone

Have you previously, or are you now, in a relationship of which you are alone even in the presence of this supposed love of your life, whom you love and they claim that they love you, but now . . . the only time you hear the word *love* used is during the act of *sex*! That's true loneliness. Please don't teach your children that this is true happiness in life. Children are quite perceptive and can sense the sadness.

So let's continue down this fork in the road alone for a moment and face this monster of loneliness. In the first movie, *Shrek*, the donkey describe it best in his deepest, darkest despair of a voice he moaned "I'm all alone!"

**Well, let's take a break. Now would be a good time for some popcorn, coke, and candy. Now before we define "alone," let's watch the movie, *Shrek*. For me, it's the two hundred and fifty-seventh time I get to enjoy it . . . later.**

Enjoy the movie? Well, if you didn't stop to watch the movie, we're already learning something about each other. Now, putting the waa, waa aside let's read what the dictionary has to state about "alone."

"Alone" is someone without help. "Alone" is someone who is by themselves. "Alone" is someone who does things single-handedly. Now, most of us do not want to be alone. And realistically, when we engage in most of the tasks of life, they seem much simpler to do when there are two or more people helping, but one clear exception to this principle is parenting. Now, don't take this wrong as if I were saying that single parenting is better than dual biological parenting. It's clearly not the best way to do all things being equal.

What we have here though in the step-on world is a failure to communicate which allows children this door to venture through and manipulate. If the child doesn't receive the desired answer to their question from Mom, then they go to Dad. Herein lies one of the big pitfalls of being a step on parent.

It doesn't take long and the children find these magic words, "You're not my mom or you're not my dad and my parent said I don't have to listen to you." May I say, "Hello, Pandora, nice to hear you." This is something that has to be hammered out early or you're heading for a major headache. There are two schools of thought for this. One thought is that the step on parent should stay out of the situation and the other thought is that this situation can be used as a tool to learn to respect adults.

Ultimately though, **the bio parent's decision rules** the roost! So move over, Mr. Rooster or Ms.Hen the wolf has arrived! Right and/or wrong, the disagreement of how to handle the current disruption doesn't get discussed in front of the children if at all possible, because there has to be order and respect. Respect has to be exemplified both ways and things may become heated.

**Now comes the real question—does the parent respect you? If not, leave while you can. This place of respect or disrespect is the place that nightmares come from.**

We've kind of gone off track. So let's journey back to alone. When we have children to look after, we are not alone, and as stated before, living our lives without a significant other can have its benefits. The biggest benefit is that there is no one to tell us that our decision, which we have made regarding our children, isn't the correct one. With their best interest in mind, this decision is our best effort. Secondly, if we are truly without help, most of us need only to get off our high horse and simply admit that we need help.

In other words, we don't need to pull some stranger off the street that we just met two months ago and now try to intertwine them into our shredded family, because they're fun and at this time they wouldn't mind playing house. Especially at first, it's much better to keep fun time separated from family time.

Predators love the easy prey. **Let's be sure that your prayers don't answer theirs.**

Remember, most of us were raised and copy someones lifestyle that influenced us. For all of us, there was at least one person that fed, clothed, and corrected us. As the parent, this comes with the parenting experience, and unlike most experiences, this one doesn't get easier per say but simply evolves overtime. The reason for this is each child has their own personality and communication style. Find out **what makes your child tick,** what makes them get up before the rising of the sun. For my children, it's going to beach to get burnt beyond human endurance. Therefore, when they find out the concequence of not heeding to your warning, it's a great opportunity to show that Mom or Dad or the adult in charge does know a little more about life than Mr. Thirteen or Ms. Thirteen with a phone. Plus the knowledge gained by you of what the children truly enjoy is leverage for lifes not so fun chores. This knowledge is invaluable as the children grow older and a swat on the butt isn't feasable any longer.

Now from who or where do we obtain assistance from in raising the children and enforcing some not so pleasant rules. Well I'll start with where you don't seek assistance. First, don't use the step on parent or potential step parent as a step stool to your entertainment. When your snuggly-poo married you, it is you they marry, not the children per se. So put that buck back in your pocket, no passing of the buck is allowed here. I thought you didn't want to be alone? Waaaa. The key word is use, if after a couple Christmases and a background check. Yes, I stated, "Get a **background check** on the new love of your life." Listen, with all the splintering of families and sexual confusion that is accepted as an excuse for people wounding others and viewing them as a victim is outrageous. **Your responsibility is to protect your family that has been endowed to you, regardless of anything that may have happened in your or their personal life. So the current pounding protector or playful**

**princess does not have alone time with the children!** *Capiche?* **Or do I have to send nine rings over for a little sit down?**

Unless, of course, they check out OK. Then it's personal discresion, but remember just because they haven't been caught doesn't mean they're OK.

Sorry for the tirade. Anyway when having to have adult alone time, pay grandma, grandpa, uncle, aunt or whomever as you would like some type of compensation for their time. Set the situation up as taking the children to the movies or something fun like that. Pizza and movies at home is a good cheap alternative. But do not drive by, kick the kids out, and let them do the "I'll tumble," for you dance as they settle in the driveway in a heap of dust at Grandma's house, again. This causes kids to feel as if they're in the way of your life. After having them your life became theirs.

# THE INNER CIRCLE

After reading some of this book thus far, hopefully there'd be some reluctance on weather or not you should bring Mr. or Mrs. Right now, who could possibly be a good candidate for the step on parent role, into your inner circle. Listen, you don't have to bring them home to the family as a candidate for marriage. If there is doubt, as there should be and as stated before, just go have fun, be romantic, and get laid if you have to. Just don't allow yourself to feel guilty for having fun as you keep the children separated from Mr. or Mrs. Right now and your dastardly dance of bedroom Disneyland. Let me digress. Did I mention that it will be very beneficial to you and the family of yours if you do not do crazy bed dance until matrimony. I know I said get laid, **but that's if you have to**. **The point is nobody** "has to have the release of love," scratch that, the release of fifty court dates, "I'm not sure who the Father is, Mom, I'm pregnant . . . again, let's kill another baby, I can't believe this is happening to me, test the other five guys first . . . Romp in the sack."

Are you seeing the picture a bit clearer now? Just one eighteen second mishap, oopps, or did I take my pill today?, can cause eighteen years of everyone involved being ripped off of a stable home. Let's not play house, because the Brady bunch not only took two parents to manage but a dog, a house keeper too, plus Sam, the butcher. And as fun as it may seem to watch and laugh at a life like that, to live the step life **will be** draining to the spirit, body, and soul.

And also from what I remember, they didn't have to deal with Mr. or Mrs. Ex and whose weekend it is this week, and "Mom lets me stay up all night at her house, and Grandma said I didn't have too, Tommy's mom lets him," blah, blah, etc.

# Step One Would you like to Dance?

One comparison I like to use when explaining this lifestyle is to compare it to slow dancing. The interactions that take place are all lighthearted and fun until someone gets their foot stepped on, or they go left when you go right, or you attempt to take the lead out of turn. In fact, some dances may lead to swapping some things that you may not want to be part of. Ugh! Seriously though, much like dancing, the more work, dedication, practice, resilience, sacrifice, and utmost commitment we exude when engaged in this moment of musical quandry, the more fun we'll experience in the long run. Similarly, like a marathon or iron man competition, all relationships and interactions of life have varios mental trials. The better that we are prepared going into the challenge, the better that the chance is that we'll come through it victorious. The biggest difference here is that we are not the only victors of our preparedness, but our children will be also. What follows is another example of insanity within sanctity.

The relationship of the step life is uniquely challenging, but it seems as simple as basic math, so let's take a look. Basic addition is one plus one, which equates to two, or in life, two experiences that have to be melded into one. But follow along as we try deciphering the mathematics needed for adding just one child's experience to the equation of our wedding decision into step life or melding of lives. Here we go.

You take one of the children's experiences which equates to one, then add one (you) which equates to two on the simplest level. OK, are you already lost on the math of one plus one equals two? If so, please review second grade math. Done? Good. Each part of the situation stands on its own. The child's view is one. The adult's view of the situation is another. But the variable is, the situation has merit of its own. Can you say algebra? So we're not done. Break out the pencils, we also have their mom's or dad's input combined with their child's interaction which equates to two on its own, plus the child's interaction combined with their mom's or dad's feedback is another two on its own, plus your interaction with Mom or Dad is another two on its own, plus Mom's or Dad's feedback to your interaction is another two on its own, plus the child's interaction with you, the step on, is two on its own. So there are approximately thirteen ways of interpreting one child's situation at this moment or vapor of time. Although the step on parent's input can be eliminated through the microscope of reality, now it's only eleven.

Realistically, life isn't basic math. The problem with life is it is like algebra, and I didn't do to well in algebra. Did you do well in algebra? The true answer is whether you're able to take the intimidating $2x+X+Y=7$ and break it down to simple mathematics. Were you able to break the problem down to the simplest form? Herein lies the formula for obtaining the correct answer to the algebraic problem. Hence, the patience that it takes to use the formula to break the problem down to the simplest form of mathematics possible is the key. Similarly, the roadblock for the transition of problem to solution in the step life is usually going to be patience practiced by . . . you. The unknowns involved in the aforementioned problem is you or me. Our baggage, our agenda, our emotion, the problem becomes more about us and our wants. Instead of us just dealing with what's before us using basic math, we often turn the problem into algebra. Our focus needs to constantly be refocused on how various dilemmas can be used to mold this child into an **outstanding, contributing, and caring adult.**

Also, reflecting a bit, this situation of television Brady bunch make believe, step life, didn't include the variable called the ex-significant other that is in most cases despised now. Even though, the ex-significant other was someone who couldn't be lived without less than a year ago when you were trying to keep the family together. Furthermore, we have to wonder if this lifestyle is so crazy for a full-grown adult to handle, how much more so for a child who only knows inherantly that they are supposed to be the center of the universe?

The commitment of the adults in charge has to be for the cohesiveness of the family as a unit, not the division of the family based on your opinion of right or wrong. Understand, as stated earlier, don't take it personal, but if you're the step on parent, you've joined their life, and the family's way of life wins. Even if the math doesn't seem to add up to the correct answer, you must accept it. Yet, there are some relationship desolvers and that's why you're reading this book before executing the I do date of destiny. The icebreakers for standing your ground are ; life and death decisions, drug/alcohol abuse, verbal/physical abuse or infidelity for any reason. Yes, even if they were accidently in the suite going to the bathroom and they tripped and while falling, their clothes went flying off. Then the sheets miraculously flew open wide as they stumbling over the shoes and ended up . . . Well you finish the scene. Now, if these issues come up, step back and ponder this. If my child were involved with someone that had these lifestyle traits, would I advise them to stay and play or run from the fun. Adult decisions aren't the funnest to make at times, but if you truly don't want to live in insanity you have to change your decision making process now. As Grandma often stated, **"Life is drama with the mama, not mathematics with the man."**

# Public Intoxication Are You within the Limits?

So are you ready for a bong load yet, a shot of alcohol or maybe about seven Vicodin? Understand this, to be a solid foundation for the children to build their lives on, we must implement a standard of which to measure our progress by (Plus have easy access to a lot of recreational drugs and alcohol), OK, skip the alcohol, I'm joking. Put that bong down too!!!! Now missy!!

In fact, since we're on this subject and on this walk of heartache and great reward, I recommend no alcohol or drugs be used because of the damage and drama it fosters in people's lives, plus the spousal abuse, child abuse, adulterous affairs, *Oh*! And of course, the "I have to apply for a third mortgage now because of court costs due to the sobriety check, stupid police!. Borrow money from her parents because our home is in foreclosure." Sorry, I can't be at my son's or daughter's recital at school, because I drove my car into a police officer while under or over the influence of drugs!

It is imperative that you understand that irregardless of the type of ass you are in the world of adulthood, your children's view of you, until they reach their mid-teens anyhow, is similar to that of God. And in their lives, to an extent, you are the closest thing to that. Ya, you. Did you hug them today? Play a game with them? Tell them that the picture they drew and whatever they told you **was great?**

# Take Time to Focus

Stepping away... listen, if you think a good kisser, backseat extracurricular activity, Mr. Right or Mrs. Right, now is a true candidate to help promote a family atmosphere in the home, let the true picture of what's before you come into focus.

Definitely not days, weeks, or months, but a true amount of time, two Christmases, a couple Easters before heavy interaction with the family. Take note, if the person you're looking to bring in stride with your family is already a drunk or druggie, do you think that beyond the party seen they are much good for anything? Listen, I joked a bit about alcohol and drugs, but truthfully, neither of those things can bring true happiness. **And their destruction is well documented**. Personally, I lost a brother and brother-in-law before age nineteen. Another brother has been crippled since he was seventeen. A couple years later, another brother-in-law ... died. I can't preach to the choir because I may still have a glass of this or that on occasion, but I can tell the director of the choir to keep close tabs on the influence that he allows this lifestyle to have.

It may sound a bit ridiculous, but to ask someone to sacrifice what may be a huge part of their lives isn't fair. I mean some people to an extent are very responsible in doing illegal activity but to demand of your children that they be exposed to the illegal activity and destabilization of there lives is a lot less fair. You see they don't have a choice of who you impart into there lives of which they will look up to. This doesn't mean, that you allow the aforementioned stud or studdette to come over after partying elsewhere either, once bltzed. That is the same thing as them partyiing at the house. It's this embrassing lifestyle that causes the children to be more courious about it. In fact, if you have the intoxicated individual drive over once under the influence, it shows total self centeredness on your part. There is no more participation in this lifestyle. You must demand for them to not participate in that lifestyle any longer . . . . stop your chaos or adopt your children out.

B.C. ( Before the year of my Lord)

Before I was married, the second time, every holiday had at the very least, alcohol involved even if we had to sneak it into our cokes, or literally we would have a keg in the car we drove. It wasn't a question if we had alcohol, but how much and where was the closest store? I was totally influenced by those who raised me. At first I rebelled against this drug and alcohol life, and that sounds good, then came the time I thought I was missing out on something. My routine at age eighteen, which was the legal age to drink in NY at the time, on Fridays I was out of school at three, walk to the bar by three forty-five, blasted drunk by 6:00 p.m.

Why am I stating this? It's because drinking was a part the life of what I identifide as life at the time. I loved my uncle who had adopted me into his family, and oh ya, he was an alcoholic. My step parent was an ex heroin addict, pot smoking, alcoholic whose contribution to our lives was teaching us to live on the streets. THE PROBLEM IS HE DID IT LITERALLY. He did finally kick heroine, but not until I got to pound on his chest at 11 years old because he had stopped breathing and was convulsing with puke going everywhere. His advice for drugs was, pot okay if its free, but don't waste your money on it. If by chance I did use heroine be sure to tap the syringe in order to get all the air out. Air in the injection could kill me, . . . . thanks but . . . no.

Listen, when I reflect back on my own stupidity I realize that I was just simply doing what was engrained in me as part of my experience of what life was and you may be doing similar. Not until I started to investigate some of my families past did I get to view this thread of divorce and abuse in my family tree. As a pastor once stated, "simply one fallen head guiding another fallen head." So if you have someone like this or it's you that is like this, it's better to figure out what your responsible for in life instead of dragging the children through what could easily add more tragedy to their already chaotic lives.

Do you remember, you and your ex's personal Fourth of July, Independence Day celebration, when finally, the judge set you all free. Your children don't need another divorce and all of its drama. It's bloody, brutal, and unforgiving. Don't put your children back into a mealy called the mosh pit of your life. I know it may sound sexually bleak, but life is not about you any longer. In order to break the cycle that has already been implanted into your childrens existence alcohol and drugs cannot be a part of daily life. In order to allow them the opportunity to thorouhgly screw up their own lives, you must give them every oportunity to have your full attention and a focused slate. Doesn't mean you can't go to movies, bowling, etc. with adults only, as stated before, just date separately from the fantasy of a family dream. Take real time to get to know the person that you'll be exposing to your children . . . . This statement can't and won't be stated enough in this book.

This is why it is best to stay sober and single to raise your children, and therefore, you'll be fully available for any task at hand. **Once the children are up and out, if you feel the need for speed and to make up for lost pain, go for it. Just make sure you remove the possibility of a, oops! baby. Simply cut the tube or slice the sack at forty-seven, you don't need waa!**

# Safeguards of Slowing Down

### So is it possible to safeguard our family?

The first step of security is to slow down, don't marry too soon or have a bedroom buddy that the children get to call Mommy or Daddy until the next Mommy or Daddy arrives. This lifestyle is the very essence of the step generations ability to thrive, if we as a nation simply stopped this act of meeting them, bedding them, and spreading them, almost immediately our nation would start on the victory trail of success.

Furthermore, as mentioned earlier, prioritize and get involved in the children's lives. Then your time will be well spent being involved with them as it should be. Ex. Baseball, band, choir, Cub Scouts, and Girl Scouts, etc.

However, if you're dead set on marriage, let it be pure dating, no mating, no birthday two way masturbating, no New Year's banging, no sex on the sidelines unless it's with yourself. No naked shows of pleasure either. Even Adam, who walked with God, ate of the fruit.

The measurement of commitment is told through the commitment of which we measure ourselves by. Listen closely, there is a code of life which your stud or studette lives by, it's their core beliefs, everyday attitudes, and frustrations. It is all around you. What jokes are funny to them? Do they enjoy seeing people be made jokes of and laughed at? You or your children could be the next joke. What sets them off in angry emotion? **(Warning . . . If you haven't seen their bad side, then you haven't seen who they're capable of being).** You will be allowing them to be an influence to your children's development. What are they willing to tolerate in everyday life give it a year or two? You must understand that if you do not play the emotional sexually stimulated game of, "I'm committed to someone's game of bang me until all your shots are fired," that you'll be able to have clarity on decisions made, and on how you want your children's lives to go.

As stated before, this isn't the Brady bunch, and this decision teaches your children how to live their lives. Also, they are reinforced that even though Mom and Dad didn't make it, the marriage commitment isn't a "mirage" commitment but a journey for a lifetime. And they, the children, being a great addition that came out of the marriage, the failed house playing, or one night stand, are now the valued commitment that your actions and decisions are focused on their needs.

# Respect for Self, Children, and the Ex

## *Respect*

Respect defined in the dictionary is as such: to revere, to esteem, to follow, to admire, it is to "act," to do something in alignment with something else. To the step on parent, everyday life brings out the worst and the best in all of us. Make sure that your worst isn't wounding those around you, and that you're part of the healing process when you do interact with those in the family that you are joining. If most of what you do is bring pain to the family, then like a flame in the fire you'll be dealt with very cautiously and superficially.

**Remember that the step on parent is often seen as the "Knight in shining armor" or the "Princess of promise."**

And the reality is that, we or you are neither. So, as stated earlier, people will discuss the burps and farts that we leave behind, more than the good times we participated in. Basically, it comes down to how we affect the children. **In their eyes, everyday life is looked upon as a first date, our best behavior is demanded.** What we did yesterday is truly gone, and what we do today measures this moment. More women should demand to be treated, as each day is another opportunity, to show and give love, or as in this case, respect, to the step on and vice versa.

Remember, enfatuated love only lasts so long, friendship only lasts so long, sex not as long as we hoped, but respect will last a lifetime. So don't think that just because you bed Mommy or Daddy that the children will think that you're God's gift to orgasmic evolutional happiness. That doesn't have any real barring on their lives. Simply the children don't even know what that is nor do they care. And as stated before, if we are currently sexually active with mr. or ms. right now, then we're going to stop, . . . "stop what?" you may ask.

**If you want to find true commitment, then stop all sexual contact below the neck/shoulders, definitely the belt line**.

During the dating scene, conservatism will save buckets of tears and turmoil in the future. And maybe even your children may learn how to respect themselves. Also, if you show value toward the child producing partner Mom or Dad, they will usually value you. **It's just a thought.**

Realize this that you may even be a psychologist with many answers of life, how to bring up grades, deal with negative attitudes, but children really don't care about much beyond the here and now. All they want is food and their way, and then, when they're sixteen . . . the car keys with a full tank of gas in the car.

Respect by the children toward the child producing partner, can be hard to read sometimes. How much more so to show respect to a perfect stranger that nobody really knew until last Fourth of July, New Year's party or Christmas bash? Ultimately, in the end, their respect that they exhibit for the step on parent, the step on parent will have to earn, but the step on parent's respect for the step children, the step on parent will have to give. Ya, you'll have to respect a mouthy fifteen year old. How's that for a good morning?

Being the step on parent, you must never forget that these beautiful children are the love of their parent's lives . . . *Oh, ya*, I almost forgot to mention, that due to this microwave age of we want it now fast frolicking bedtime fun, where the only work or comittment is to tear off the clothes without cutting up the carrots. You'll not only marry your current passionate love of your life but the ex-love of their life, plus his or her family. hip hip hor—hey what the? The ex. on some level is now a part of your family tree . . . forever. If your next response is hip hip no! It may be time to go. If your response is yeaaah!, I'll see you at the tree planting cerimony.

# Do you have All the Answers?

## Leave the Comparisons at the Door

Comparing yourself to that ex-significant, make them scream in ecstasy all night: lover, husband, wife, boyfriend, girlfriend, Mom, Dad, dumb ass whatever words are used to best describe them is irrelevant, simply put, do not allow competition to evolve toward them. **I'll repeat, don't compete.** And don't let the family pull you into that heartbreak trap. Because, as mentioned pages back, it's only a matter of time before you get to hear the dreaded anti-step on parent statement of all time, you're not my mom and or dad. And forget trying to be their parent because **it's true your not and you never ever will be**. You must understand that if you earn their love and respect, those closest to the situation know it and you'll never have to claim those treasured emotions, because you've already justified your place through their words of acknowledgment and appreciation.

Ask any parent and they'll admit that there are fewer statements that hurt as much as when you hear your children acknowledge someone else in their heart as Mom or Dad; it's a truth that twists the inner soul.

As a parent who abandoned and has been replaced by a pseudo parent, they'll finally realize, after they blink, what they have done. In the child's eyes and heart that other person **has earned** the title that they would have been fortunate enough to inherit. Or quite possibly, the children are just being brats and are now manipulating whomever through guilt to goad them into buying something that the child wants.

Oh, well, at least now mom or dad are getting laid by some hunk or honey. The bottom line is respect has to be earned.

Now, to assess what we've just read and whether or not we should put down this book again and head for the hills, the answer is heck, yea, unless you're an egotistical, controlling masochist, which, by the way, I am/was but have had the opportunity to confront and work on all of these shortcomings. Thanks to my, well, their children. I've learned through the patience of my wife and the backside of her children that family is not about you, I, or me, but we.

And a whole heck of a lot of "we" especially if you're French. We, madam. Yes, dear.

**Disclaimer (No actual backsides were damaged during this lifestyle interaction)**

# Are you an ECM

Here's a quick check to see if you possess at least one of these personality problems in order to step into something that you may attempt to remove from your shoe later.

**Egotist:** An Egotist would look at this situation and state, "I can do it."
**Control freak:** A control freak would state, "Lay down some laws and all will be OK."
**Masochist:** A masochist would be beaten bloody, then state, "That's all you got, let's do it again."

Basically, an egotist does great as long as they're seen as great.
A control freak does great as long as people remain in control.
And a masochist will remain as long as they get to endure pain. *Welcome to the house of pain.*

Truthfully though, most of us, who would embrace such an idea as taking on someone else's life with all the loose ends and drama, must have psychological problems of our or their own. This is one of the main contributing factors for the continuation of the breakdown of the family unit and birth of the step generation. At least half of us are from broken homes, and the other half at least knows of someone who is. This causes the wounded souls of many to try and do something many of us haven't even had the experience of living in ourselves. Thus the degeneration of our nation continues. And the step generation lifestyle continues to be embraced more and more as the norm.

Being that the family as an initial unit has been destroyed, tending to the collateral damage to the children has to be job one. We must stabilize the home. Once again the person you're dating, and hopefully not mating with, cannot be a control freak because one of the best inspirations of the human spirit is uncertainty, and if they're constantly teaching, safety only comes in certainty; your children remain childlike even into adulthood. If the person is an egotist, that's not good, because of the obvious that in the family, life is not about you or I but we. And finally, if they show signs of masochism, this can have its positive influence, but to teach the children that enduring unhealthy pain is OK isn't good either. We all have thresholds to endure in life, but to have your children deal with excess pain so you can have sexual gain is not fair to them. *Sad.*

# Whose Turn Is It?

Did I mention that most patched-together, second-time-around marriages only have a one—to three-year shelf life? Consequently, we, you, them, him, her, and I am the role models to our children. Therefore, if we sleep with this person, date that one, and see this one every three months, we end up modeling a turnstile type of existence for our children to model their lives after. It's kind of like having McDonald's food constantly. Yes, the food is fast and flavorful, but it lacks nutrition. Minerals and vitamins are nutrients for the body. This is like stability and sanity being the foundation to the family. Many different inputs are needed. But whatever is going to be ingested has to be usable for maintenance, re-building and healthy energy. So within our family however we arrange it, if we remove the opportunity to teach courage in the face of fire, then the ability to teach how to stand up to challenges in life is lost. As a result, when we divorce, marriage has lost its intrinsic value, and the binding identity for people to unify under a common cause is crushed. The reason for this is we are showing our children that life is about the self and like people in a sinking boat most give up on the boat as soon as the boat takes on water and their asses start getting wet. Instead of everyone working a bit harder to patch the problem and remove the water. They abandon ship in search of another in the ocean of life. The problem is in a storm all boats take on water. Here is another analogy using the boat: When the storms of life come and they will, don't be headstrong and row the boat of your life into the storm. Courage and determination are great traits to teach. But also patience and perseverance have just as much if not more value. Find ways to use the storms of your life to drive the boat where you need to be. Sometimes nature and God will do all the work for you. In the step life, you often have to go the long way through patience in order to survive the storms. And the truth is that all storms do reach a point of dissolving and subside. Now, you can stand in a whole new day.

# I Knew This Day Was Coming

Thus, when we face our storms of life, of which there will be plenty of opportunity to show the real you, and the human capacity of exhaustion is reached for the knight in shining armor or princess of promise, we're left with the flesh-and-blood person. This person who has to put their pants on one leg at a time, and when they get sick like the rest of us during flu season, we now don't know how and more importantly they don't know how to react.

You see, a princess can only balance on a pedestal so long before enough of the pedestal is chipped away by those of envy and hate, then the princess falls. The knight can only face so many dragons before he realizes he can't defeat them all without help.

So most of the stresses of you and your children's lives have to be dealt with by you, don't pass the responsibility to the step on parent because they married you . . . Extracuricular responsibilities are done by the biolodgical family. Doctor, dentist, baseball, dance, karate, etc. Please. Keep in mind that they married you because they loved you. The children and all the drama, they couldn't have calculated if they had to. Yet does this ignorance dismiss their responsibility as an adult in the situation? No. **Although it is your responsibility to be as honest and forthcoming to them with the full scope of the situation that they're stepping into,** the real reason that you don't go out on Thursday is because the ex comes over for dinner. Birthdays and holidays are spent for a moment under one roof for the children's sake of some semblance of family. Saturday mornings aren't step class workout but a sex with the ex. Workout, . . . . hey, it's still a workout, right? In all honesty, some or all of these aforementioned may have bearing on the adult you're dating and who may be stepping into this chaotic life. The future is unknown, but yesterdays life will probably be much like tomorrows life until some changes are made today.

# Please Don't Step On My Toes

As stated earlier, the step on parent coming into the family situation simply wants love from their spouse, just like the children do, but your spouse is their mom or dad. The one thing that has to be absorbed into the essence of the step on parent though is that the children get the love through principle. They do not have to earn anything from Mom or Dad and definitely not you. Ewww! It is life as it is or actually should be. There cannot be a sense of competition between the step on parent and the children. Thus, the term "step on parent" is used to describe the adult involved that will be a second-class citizen in this family.

## Doesn't that sound just peachy?

If you *can't handle the fact*, *the fact* that you'll be number two in the parent's heart and you'll be number two in the children's heart, then the number one thing to do is leave.

A wise man once said, "The battles of war are romanticized, but the stories are written with real blood." DAB 2008

# THE PRICE FOR ADMISSION

## Can You Handle Being Stepped On?

As the degeneration of family structure spreads like cancer, our livelihood —as we know it—dies too. Cancer kills its self during it's consumption of its host.

Marriage is a human drive in life, but it's been lost in the mirage of self-seeking satisfaction causing severe destabilization of democracy.

Do not marry only for yourself and happiness, but for your children and humanity. Regardless of your motivations as a parent to make a family, whether your choice of a childbearing partner was a good one or a bad one, the impact it has on your child's interpretation of life is irreversible.

Remember that no matter how harsh truth is, truth can be dealt with.

Partial truths, also known as manipulating lies, can only enhance the confusion of the paradox children view as marriage today.

Most great superpowers of history had, for a time at their core, a family structure. And once this structure, whether moral or not in some views, had deteriorated, so to the society it bore soon fell from greatness to mediocrity or worse.

Some people are of the opinion that mothers and fathers that have dissolved their marriages should stay in a state of nonmarital suspension until the children involved are grown. This opinion has great wisdom as far as if there were two parents involved with the children as priority one, but obviously this isn't the case because many families are now in disarray due to the lack of commitment to the children's lives, and people staying focused on their wants

With any luck, as a person studying this possible step lifestyle, you'll have to have the courage to be honest with yourself and the other person involved in order to understand this undaunted, unappreciated, and unthankful task that you will be walking hand in hand into.

Whether a self-centered Mother or Father join you in this experience of the step on life, you must understand that their perception of your needs will be about as good as your perception of their needs. The bottom line is if you aren't willing, at least for the children, to honor the vows that you and their parent willingly took before your *creator, friends, and family,* then do not marry, and definitely, do not move in, and do not pass go or collect two hundred dollars.

Developmentally, the children don't get the marriage thing nor, more importantly, do they care. Marriage seems to bring more chaos than clarity at this point in their lives.

**Take time to read the definition of martyr. Then insert your name where the word *martyr* exists. This has to be your experience in this lifestyle. Can you handle it?**

Remember this, their parent is usually more focused on being the good guy in the children's lives more so than teaching the good life. Most anything good in life comes at a price and the parent usually isn't willing to pay the price of teaching.

As mentioned earlier, once someone is respected by someone that tag of respect stays intact for that person, and it would take an extreme act of disruption or disloyalty to change that opinion. Now, why is that? It's because it takes work to gain respect. It takes victory in the the face of adversity to gain respect. More importantly though is the fact that respect isn't a feeling but an act of allegiance earned. People in general act out of emotion and the moment. Those that don't live on the magic mountain thrill ride of emotion learn to find the real motives that drive those they interact with more quickly. Simply, I can't count on both hands the young men that showed up at our house with back seatidous , that weren't seen at our house again once they were invited over to the house and not allowed to leave the living room unless it was to go to the bathroom, kitchen, or front door. No going into our daughters room even if the door was open, because the door seem to accidentally get closed on occasion. Sorry dad, oh ya, and why is the pillow on his lap? I'm sure I don't need to paint the picture for you that comes out of our children being alone at home with their best friend, much less the opposite sex.

Now, of coarse, there are exceptions. It's just that the fact remains our job is to protect them from anything that may thwart them from having the best opportunities in life to succeed with the minimal amounts of stress, even if it's simply there own ignorance. Now, will this type of act be a popular rule to live by in the house. No, but it will save some innocence, heart ache, and possibly you from having to deal with your child being directly involved in an abortion decision without your consent. Can we say thirteen anyone? If by chance you've had to deal with this subject you realize the affect it has lasts a life time.

Finally, this type of parenting is simply the emotional cost that has to be paid in order to keep order, and more importantly, teach order, plus respect. The reaction will vary from different children. The reality hits when one of their classmates shows up with a pregnancy pouch or a friend that swore that they would never have this happen to them is now working every night and weekends to pay for the frolick on free love street. Or, more likely, she's left alone and he's now dating her friend. Owwweeee

# Youngsters Don't Think

Dateline 2007: Children stalked by perverts on the Internet. Who's at fault? Is it the pervert? Is it the child? Is it the Mom? Is it the Dad? Is it Grandma? Is it Grandpa? Is it MTV? Is it no TV? Is it baseball? Is it the first lady? Is it the president himself?

Truth can be known, it really doesn't matter. There are predators in all aspects of life. From relatives to priests, to congressmen (the term "men" used loosely), to Moms and Dads these sick people seem to be in abundance. If you doubt that this is fact, just punch in a zip code and check for the predatory pedophiles or domestic abusers in your neighborhood or better yet his or hers. So before you introduce those who would be at a disadvantage to those of power, *think*!

Your children totally rely on your discretion as a parent to only allow certain things or people in their lives which **they as children should benefit from**. It takes a lot of time to really get to know someone and their potential to hurt or commit unacceptable and irreversible acts toward others. Mr. or Ms. Potential Step On may be lifted high on your pedestal, but your beautiful, innocent children will test those who enter the family circle. First, we are commanded to protect. Then we can play.

Also when it comes to your children, the children view all of those people who would steal your precious time from them as more of a threat than a toy. Even if they are cool, these people will be challenged in ways that they never expected. **Don't risk you or your child's life for a good time, which could have negative affects for a lifetime.**

# Holidays Are a Hoot

The festivities are beginning, the family has gathered around, and all the food has been prepared. Ahhh, the holiday season is such a great time to come together and celebrate family! Uncle him, aunt her, and cousin somebody from some place all come together to share food, drink, and fun. But for the child who has had their family disassembled as they knew it, for many, this time of year becomes a real bummer. Before I sought counseling and started being counseled on issues in my life, I didn't even think about the holiday season one way or another. As I look back though until I was well into adulthood, holidays were hollow days. This was the time of year that I was shuffled here and shuffled there. I received some of the stuff and smiled a lot. Yet something wasn't right.

Not until I got my own step life going with my own stepchildren did I revisit the insanity that most in this situation live.

At first, it was just another holiday of going here and there. Then I realized, this is my life with my family. Not my parents. Not my sisters. not my brothers. grand parents whatever? So my next question was, how would I like to celebrate the holidays if I were a child again? The answer was as follows: With my mom and dad at home with the dog playing in the gift wrap and dinner cooking all day. Being able to go out and play with my friends with my new toys. So, this is how we attempt to do Christmas and holidays each year. Outside family gets remaining time or rescheduled time. Rescheduled means a weekend before or after the said holiday. In our situation the children are at the other child producing partners house on the eve of Christmas. Christmas day is spent at home. Thanksgiving is swapped each year, etc. it works for the adults . . . it sucks for the kids.

# Hammering Out the Holidays

## Unhappy Holidays

One of my first memories as a child was Christmas morning with my new family that had adopted me. I woke up really early, the sun wasn't even up and I went out to see if Santa had come to my house. Lo and behold! There was Santa putting stuff under the tree. And I don't mean my dad dressed up as Santa but Santa the red-suited revolutionary who believed all children should have at least one toy. I got a train that whistled and a basketball hoop that I couldn't shoot through without the help of my pop. I was about four or five at the time. This act of holiday happiness would be my dream for all children.,. Each holiday should be spent surrounded by the security and sanctity of home.

My next memory is not as rosy as I lost my home, my dog, my sister, and my life just as I was starting to adapt to it. My mom and I now embarked on our life and journey through the birth pains of a sexually revolutionized society I call the step generation. The year was 1966. And my holidays would not be much fun from then on. You have got to understand when Dad picked me up, he wanted me to be cleaned up and respectable. Mom thought that it was better if I represented the Beatles and the song revolution. So while she was off experimenting with the yellow submarine, my golden locks were being cut off and I was embarrassed no matter where I was each weekend. It sucked!!!

Now to address some of the happy holiday hindrances, communicate. Yep, the one thing that neither one of you ex's as a couple were able to do very good is the one thing your children need most from you two. **Now isn't that a quandary?** Now don't get defensive, please.

Ultimately, all the children want to do is enjoy both of you. Ya, both of you are the most important thing to them. Don't use them to further your war on this 1$#*@(&*^&%$# situation. Whoever is the weekend visiting parent has to grow up and understand the child's point of view. Outside of the ninety-six hours a month that they spend with you, they have five hundred and seventy-two hours of life without you or your direct input on life. Their reality is where they live, not where they visit like Disneyland every other week. It is understandable that as an abandoning parent you miss your children, but in their eyes whose fault is that? So be understanding with them, because your happy-holiday gift to whoever the person is that is under you now, they could really careless about. Consequently, you two ex's may not have been able to have reached a compromise between yourselves when you were deeply in love and married or worse just doing the nasty until . . . oh/oops happened, but now you better reach some sort of agreement, or your children won't follow either one of you in time. In reflection though, that may not be such a bad idea.

Your next question may be:

What the !$#%^&%*)()$ do you mean unhappy holidays? Even in the worst of families, holidays are the one time during the year that we gather and reminisce about the previous year just to look on to our future, right?

Not so for the stepchild who would have to walk at least 1,257 steps just to ask a question of Mom or Dad. And that's only if Mom or Dad were smart and stayed in the neighborhood and now lives two blocks away. This, of course, is in sharp contrast to the child in an intact home with Mom or Dad being downstairs or down the hall. I'll give an example through a story of Mary and Frank, the beginning of the unhappy holidays/birthdays of the step life.

The holiday/birthday stepping-stones of the step-generation child's logistical life are as follows:

This story is entitled: the Unhappy Holidays of the Step Life.

Once upon a time, Mary and Frank were married, had three beautiful children—Thomas, Kristine, and Barbara, then they lived unhappily ever after. Thomas was named after his grandfather on his mother's side. Kristine was named after Frank's great-aunt, who didn't have children. And Barbara with beautiful golden locks, who was said to have received the golden locks from the Spanish ancestry of her mother, was named after, well, no one, because it was said that she would blaze her own path in life and be the one that the following grandchildren would be named after.

Well, ever after was moving along well. Then Frank frankly found out that Barbara's golden locks were actually from a surfer named Sam, who taught private surf lessons at women's spa in Baja California.

Now, the way that Frank found this out isn't really as important as Mary admitting that Sam had given her private lessons on how to ride the board. She even received a certificate recognizing her overall effort and commitment to learning how to ride. It's on display in the bathroom. A mishap moment that results in marrital mayhem.

So, now, what does happily ever after, Grandpa, Spain, great-aunts, and a spa in Baja have to do with the step generation? Well, as 50 percent of our nation's marriage fall apart in our self-absorbed, self-satisfying society called America, the unity and perseverance required to maintain marriage is a lost art form as the cohesiveness that the battle within a marriage affords us the opportunity to grow through is dissolved. So as this basic training of sacrifice is not afforded to our youth, our youth mirror the self-seeking attitudes that have been taught.

Once again, what does any of this have to do with great-aunts, Grandpa, Baja, or holidays?

Once this unity of family is broken, all the pieces become more susceptible to deterioration and destruction. Sad to say, but Mary and Frank did not survive the truth about Barbara's locks. And Thomas, Kristen, and Barbara began their journey of the hopeful yet unhappy holiday/birthday life of the step generation.

You see, when Mom and Dad went to court to figure out what to do with the house that Mom had just redecorated and the minivan and convertible that Dad had just purchased, not to forget the pool table, the sixty inch flat screen, the couch, the curtains, the cat, and the dog or dogs. Oh, and last but not least who, what, and where of the children?

Mom had to work now. Dad would need to continue working. The children had school, dance, baseball, and gymnastics. But did they need it?

Dad had to move and Thomas was told he had to leave his house, and mom, and sisters to go live with Dad.

At first, this change didn't seem to be too bad to Thomas, except he couldn't take his dog peanut with him.

The girls got to stay home with mom, except no more bedtime stories by Dad and peanut seemed to follow them around everywhere.

Now Thomas's birthday came up, and the birthday wasn't the same as when Mom and Dad were together. First, there was no cake baking when Thomas got up to go to school. Second, he thinks his dad would have totally forgot about his birthday had Grandpa not called and reminded him by wanting to talk to Thomas to wish him a Happy Birthday!

Well, Frank wasn't very happy that Mary's dad, whom he wasn't too fond of anyhow, had called, and what came next?

Frank's new girlfriend picking up the phone as Mary called? Meanwhile, Frank only caught the end of Thomas's conversation with Grandpa as he stated, "Sure, Grandpa, come on over. I'll be here after school."

Now, as a child, that this family holiday and celebration could be a problem wasn't even conceivable to Thomas, his grandpa had never, as long as Thomas could remember, missed his favorite grandson's birthday party. As Dad lectured Thomas on the differences of life now, Mom called, and the nightmare on Dad's street began. The children didn't understand, and the parents didn't seem to care.

A simple celebration of a birthday kicked off a never ending and downward spiraling effect of the step life's unhappy holidays.

The saddest part of the children's reality was that they didn't ask for any of it! The lost bedroom, the lost game room, the lost TV room, the lost dining room, the lost yard, the lost best friend, the lost security, and the addition of, "them"—the person now kissing my parent. They were all part of Mom's and Dad's great scheme of escape. And sadly, the children are the biggest losers.

So when the families are splintered through divorce or inappropriate self-serving lifestyles, the situation has to be magnified in order to see all the players clearly.

During this magnification process, we see all players that have affected this unit of humanity called the family. And within the splinters, we'll find those who were committed to themselves more than the unit called the family. Many times, we all want to point fingers and blame, but the last I knew it takes two to fight.

# Preparing For a Glamorous Garden

Whether we step, stomp, or pull weeds, weeds need to be dealt with or they'll ruin the whole garden is what my grandmother used to say. So when we pull two, three, or four direct families together and expect them to yield a good life for all involved, we must realize the work that will be demanded of us. Having a stepfamily can also be compared to having a garden.

Weeds are the distruction of anything that would normally nurture our garden. In the beginning of a garden, we have to take unlike items, blend them together, and somehow expect them to produce worthwhile results. I mean, dirt is content being dirt. Water is content being water. Poop is poop, and a seed is fine dwelling within itself.

All of these separate items don't necessarily need the other to survive; yet when we put them all together in the proper proportions, they produce life. The most damaging effect of the step life is the inappropriate division of the time of all who are involved. Time is the water of the garden. The problem lies in the fact that we only have one hose to water this garden of partiality. That hose is Dad or Mom. So once again I'll state, if you're not adding to the growth of this garden, you're choking it as a weed steals water and nutrients. So step aside or get stepped on.

The number one key to understanding a healthy step house is proportion, time equates to love in the life of a child, and Moms and Dads are responsible to deliver it. Love is like nutrients, and all aspects of it are needed for a healthy family. Remember that the prisons are full of people whose parents gave them just enough attention to survive, and from there they were left on there own to find security, fun, and family. Most, if not all gang members, refer to their gang as their family.

**I state our job as parents isn't maintaining surviving but teaching thriving.**

Back to the garden, as a garden grows so does its need for certain water and nutrients and the delivery of the proper amounts. Some plants, or children, demand a higher amount of love to sustain health. Others need only to know that you are there when needed in order to remain content. Also, if you as a parent aren't there to maintain the garden, how would you ever know what it needs? If there are weeds choking the cucumbers out, who will be there to decide if the tomatoes need to have a stake now in order to sustain stability? Are the carrots and potatoes receiving too much water and now they are rotting, or are the radishes not receiving enough water? And so it goes.

You see, if we divide too much time to ourselves and others, we don't give the garden "that we planted" a chance to become the best it could be, but rather the garden becomes whatever dominates the dirt. The cucumbers will look like weeds because they found security in the overwhelming cover of the weeds. The tomatoes look like weeds also because they lacked something or someone to stabilize them, and therefore, they took the easy way of growth on the ground. The carrots and potatoes rotted and caused starvation to the other plants due to the inability to control the duration of time that they received the flow of water or change the way that the water was delivered.

So time equates to love, love is the nutrients of relationships, time is the delivery of such things.

Be sure to have the proper proportions and to be proactive in the provisions of your children's life. The children, much like the garden, will yield to what they are given to.

This is where we have the favorite child versus the needy child competition arising. The fact is neither child is at fault. It is the parents' responsibility to monitor time spent with each child. Not your interpretation of time spent but time spent doing something that the child would like to do. Listen, Mom or Dad, believe it or not, you will actually like one child over another just because of their personality, but it is imperative that your love for each child is clear. Clarity comes with time spent with each child. It can be intimidating, but here is where the sixteen-year-old will open up and ask some of the most embarrassing questions. Once again, when our children act up, it's time to go on a road trip. Take your daughter to your sister's house for the day. Just you two and your sister will be hanging out. If your daughter doesn't open up on the way, set aside some time for you to go to the store and leave her with your sister. She may open up there. What things do your children have to look forward to? Are you going on a family trip, going on a boat ride, going to the mall with fifty bucks to spend? What?

Let me explain something else, if you are the stepparent/adult you have to do the math and realize that the more attention that the children get from Mom or Dad, the less time that you get. This is not so bad sometimes. Go and see an old friend. Go visit Mom and Dad. Oh, sorry. I forgot your parents were divorced too. You could just stay home and pet the dog, write a book, or read a story. Whatever.

# Don't Pass on the Pity

What a shame if our children are raised in a country with all the best that life has to offer them, and we only allow them to become a carbon copy of us! Although as children they will aspire to be as we are, our job is to point them to the potential life that they may embark on. Especially with all the self-help books, pshyciatrists, and babbling broads on the radio to help challenge and guide us.

Listen, the pitfalls of life are anything that can trip the potential of our children to be the healthiest that they can be. Our commitment to our children from the first day that we have them is to expose all of the pitfalls that may want to trip up their life and keep them from climbing their mountain.

So what are some of the pitfalls that need stepping over in order to allow our children to not get tripped up in this life? Well, we always have the other child producing partner and the influence that they'll have. This could be a positive or negative influence. The choice will be yours as the parents that produced this child into this life. A hint is, don't keep your wounds of the failed relationship with the other child producing parent exposed to their everyday life. Then we have Mr. or Mrs. Step On and their baggage of life coming into this maze of mahem. Oh ya, don't forget the rambling on forever before the microwave was invented, Grandparents. Now, grandparents can be a calming source of positive influence and unconditional love ; unless, of course, they have the condition of the child sides with their side of the family or has a miserable time while exposed to them.

And my all time favorite "the cultural collision of sexual promiscuity" that was so attractive yesterday but is such a pain today. As your child rounds the corner of childhood to adolescense hopefully they've heard the standard that they'll be held to and expected to rise to in order to have any social life beyond the home. Our job is to guide and expose the pitfaalls for our children and not justify our actions in life, because they'll also find ways to justify and join in the genrational step that is destroying our nation. Then the only option we'll have is to pass on the pity.

# The Variety of Life

The variety of people in our life allows us to experience some spice. And much like the different foods in a garden with different flavors that allow unexpected palet experiences, so too, do the people that we come in contact with. Will I go down this road of the international experience? Sure, I will, and then some. Can we say religion, South American, North American, European, Asian, farmer, or city folk. We all look similar, but let me tell you that we all are very different. Our holiday interactions are different. Our marriage ceremonies are different. Our daily expectations of our spouses are different. The respect levels of our family members are different. Our root belief system is different. Our religious practices are different. Our tolerance levels are different.

When we meld together two families with similar cultural lifestyles, getting some uniformity is hard enough, but when you start to cross color, religion, or societal lines, family identity becomes harder for the children and adults involved. More importantly though is the children. If there is to be a step on parent in your children's life, I recommend staying in a similar cultural circumstance. Accordingly, if the other parent is from a Caucasian background, bring in a Caucasian step on. If by chance the child's parent is Mexican, stay with Mexican. If black, Negro, or African American, stay with a black, Negro, or African American lifestyle, Chinese, Japanese, whatever. If by chance you have a mixed child of race, keep consistent. I know this really sounds racist and shallow, and love doesn't see these things, but it really takes a special person to be transparent and understanding to cultural things. Am I sounding racist, probably? I'm just telling you, at times my kids struggle because they clearly favor skin color of another race. I'm not Indian or Mexican and they clearly are. It's just a thought before plunging into the love shack. Can people cross cultural boundries and have healthy relationships? Sure they can, but realisticaly, it adds another layer to the onion of life that the children have to deal with. Dealing with a step parent is confusing enough. Once again, it may be better just to stay single as a parent and keep the varieties of life as your own experience.

# Picking Battles

One of the most common battles that we'll face with our children or spouse concerning the children is outside basic rules of life and often start with this statement, "Mom, Dad, the step on or grandma allows me to do this activity or that activity that is in question." In other words what the child wants to do, see, or live as a lifestyle is Ok by them, another adult figure of equal or higher status in the child's view. The beginning to taming most of these types of conflicts is to have common vision of how the parents react through teamwork. With a common vision we can remove mole hills before there are mountains. Without it, mole hills are the very foundation of all these type of conflicting mountains. It's his fault, it's her fault, it's their fault. Believe me, it's all our fault for dropping the ball in the first place. Yes, even you, the step up and step in the way, step on parent.

But I digress; this is not about you or him or her but them, the children. Sit down with the ex-stud or studdette, and hammer out some agreed-upon basic rules. Listen, if the child wants pink hair, they have to wear it. If your boy likes caca pants, better known as sagging, let them know the association of the intellect that usually accompanies that clothing style—both to inform them of the perception people will have of them and safety through association, neither of which will they act like they care about, of course.

Listen, as babes in the home, babes being age two years until about eleven or twelve years old, discipline is quite easy. A simple timeout does wonders as does a nap. But adolescence is, well, I'm sure you, a, you kinda know what, 'em, well, **difficult** is a kind enough way to explain this transformational time of turmoil.

Suddenly, there is an opinion that is stated with attitude, with a deeper voice, and with less eye-to-eye contact accompanied with the shrug. This change for a parent is somewhat intimidating, but for a step on parent, it can be even more intimidating.

Therefore, teens can cause an overreaction by the step on parent to safeguard themselves by upping the ante of a argument and disciplining the child.

This is a awkward moment to say the least, ecspecially if the child was in the wrong. As a step on, you're now in their home court since you signed over your life to Mr. or Mrs. Right now. **Oh! Still not married? If this type of stress doesn't appeal to your adventurous side, I say again, "Where are the shoes, and don't let the door hit you on the backside as you bolt out of it!" Halleluiah!!!**

At first, one of two things happens as a result of the step on stepping up to shut the pup up, the step on overreacts because this isn't their child that they're speaking to or the parent now becomes the teammate of his or her baby being attacked. Thus, the statement is born by the step on parent, "Waa, I feel alone in my own home." Get used to it or/and get stepping out. The sympathy train left about thirty seconds ago. If you run fast, you may be able to catch it. Listen, Mr. or Mrs. Step on, the potential parental figure head, if your still here after all the warnings . . . Shut up, stupe!

Herein lies some of the reality of what you're in for, if you step up and step in to the arena of the step generation. How do I know? Because I'm in it. And here's some of what seven years of getting stepped on has taught me.

**Last call, all aboard!**

# Sounds Like a Fun Ride

"I'm tired of being stepped on" is what one exhausted adult stated, and then Bobby at the other end of the bar said, "Here, here." Understanding what the step on life is about is impossible because of all the variations of people's lives. But being prepared by having both you and the parent face many facts openly and honestly in the beginning is what will give you the best chance of success. Truthfully, I am a Christian, reborn into hope, faith, kindness, joy, and peace about fifteen years ago. I was working on being Christ like when I met my wife and children and I'm still working on it. When I took on this challenge, about seven years ago, I truly thought there would be praise, rejoicing, and happiness. Don't get me wrong, there was. Then the second week started . . .

Now I just realize that the praise usually has a cost attached to it. Without the teaching of Jesus Christ, I would not have had the resiliency to have made my marriage work beyond two years. This isn't time for testimony and trying to convert you to Christianity and the teachings of Jesus, but if you're really a person who wants to save some children, a man or woman from themselves and develop a place to call home, check out the Bible. It has a great way of explaining structure, and don't go to the most hated verse of the Bible by modern women like, "Wives submit," because that same point in the Bible commands men to serve there wives as Christ did for the church . . . dying to himself for the greater good of the family.

I believe that your children will thank you. Well, at least, once they have children. One last thing about church, it allows a place to go and get the focus off the "me" of the step life.

It also allows a place for the kids to be encouraged by adults that will share what's being taught with the children. If you have teens in this mess, good luck, they don't like anything.

The book of James will encourage your duty to family.
The book of Acts will show courage in the face of hostility.
1 John, all five chapters, teaches how we are loved, valued, and to value.

Still hell-bent on conquering this mountain, huh? OK then, you must not mind being a martyr (Oh, you didn't look it up earlier, well, please look it up before continuing), get some gasoline, rope, and the stake is over there with wood around it. Take your place, tie your hands, put your blindfold on, and get ready for some heat, baby.

# Good Friend Vs Good Find

## Warning Follows a Rewarding Life

"Step on parents, beware Mom or Dad" has a unique lesson to learn here, and it may cause a divorce.

As a youth growing up, we all have experienced jealousy in one way or another.

So Mommy or Daddy don't get upset here because the step on parent gets to be the good guy or gal when it comes to policing the children, or should I state, your children. Other than respect issues in this marriage, these children are your children, and the step on is not the parent. So just like the children don't have to like the step on parent, you as the parent has to like both, and that may cause you to think that you're sleeping with the enemy at times. Tip for step on parents: Don't try to win the children over or the parent over just "Shut up," "Get up," and "Shut your mouth." Sorry to inform you, but you don't get to discipline them. Mom or Dad gets to have that responsibility all to themselves. Just be an adult about things and if you're an OK person, most likely the children and parent will enjoy your company. Here's where being on the same page in disciplining is critical, therefore no matter where the children are at they get the same feed back and guidance as to what's accepted and not accepted.

As a result, the tension in the home is reduced significantly. And when Mom or Dad has to drop the hammer, who do you think they'll see as the go-to guy or gal?

Still be wary though because blood runs thicker than water, and if you're caught in its current, you will be assed out. So beware, many parents are looking to recruit a bedtime buddy to deal out the punishment. Do not fall for this task. Only misery and isolation will follow you, the step on parent. Then the parent gets to remain in friendship status with the children as you, along with the ex-stud or studette, are villainized as a controlling a—hole.

## Blood Pressure Pills, Please. Mom or Dad, This Bud's for You . . .

Friendship with our children is like cold air and hot air colliding. Sooner or later, there will be a storm. How you prepare them to handle your perspective of life will birth the outcome of the severity of the storms that will follow. If the parental guidance has been nonexistent and the child has been allowed to go out of control (In other words, you've been the buddy), the result, once discipline is dealt out, will be like a tornado with all in its path being destroyed. The good thing is now we start to rebuild.

But if the proper guidance has been taught, not only will the forces' meeting be less destructive, but at worst, there will be an annoyance more like a light summer thunderstorm with a couple flashes of lightning. The thunderstorm can be scary at times but it's wake of destruction is controlled much easier than a tornado. The sooner you realize this fact, the better. Also remember that some things you use to raise your children work generically. But your children are all individuals, and therefore, each one will give you an opportunity to use your God-given imagination to deal with them in their own unique way. Isn't that great?

Listen, if you want a loving, non-manipulative relationship with your children, as adults stay cracking until you can't crack no more. Then take a breath and start all over again.

The basic lesson is anything good gained in this life comes with a cost. The price paid here will be the innocent perception of children and the reality of life and its struggles. You and the ex have already compromised the childrens innocence. This part of their fairy tale is over already.

The good thing about children is resiliency. Being honest with them is OK. Minus the dirty details, they already lost their knight or princess. You don't have to trash your choice of a child producing partner because you couldn't handle your adult decision **to not honor your own commitment. Once again wait until the children ask about this one. Mmm, hmm, hmmm!**

Anyhow, much of the preparation that you afford your children doesn't show, until our beautiful children become the terrible teen. Dunnn, dunnn, dunnn. Teens have to be taught how to deal with the turmoil of life. There is Testosterone and tampons, first loves and homosexuality, "Their friends stay out all night and why can't I," just to name a few, it's great.

Most of these children have already had much to deal with. And hopefully, you've equipped them the best you could for this leap in life. The largest hurdle from childhood to adulthood is coming to the realization that we all are responsible for our own life's decisions. We are all responsible for our own life's decisions. We are all responsible for our lifes decisions.

I really wish it was sixteen instead of eighteen that our children become recognized as adults. Because this age is a real challenge to Mothers and Fathers who have to deal with what these adolescents want without understanding the true cost.

So we as adults must take this time with our children and view it as an opportunity to use this as a tool for teaching patience, persistence, and conquest.

**The admission price for us to raise our children is all we got and then some.**

Keep in mind, if you love them unconditionally, demand respect, and **follow through with the price they chose to pay for their actions**, it won't take long for them to figure out the dance.

# Love?

**Relatively speaking, love is simply relative.** In our culture here in America, that loves its beauty, it has all but pushed the characteristics of character out of love. Before this previous generation in our country's history, which now seems to believe that it is more important to have a job than to raise a self-sufficient family, being a family, and the character that made up that family used to matter to those directly and indirectly involved.

**The title of this section is love, and love is relative** . . . or at least the interpretation of love is relative to how you were loved as a child. This love gift from our parents is often the gift we pass on to our own children. I mean, remember the first time that you repeated a statement that your parent used to say, other than a swear word, and you had that thought, "I used to hate it when my dad or mom or stepparent would call me that or they might say this or that in front of my friends." Now here we are doing or saying that very same thing. Odd, isn't it?

Here's the measuring device that we need to use to decide if our statement is of good intent, and no, the intent of your actions or statement is not a good marker. Because we, just as our parents, may have had good intent in why we said what we did, so it's not our intent that needs to be addressed but rather our delivery of our intent or message, *huh?*

## To Connect With Our Kids, We Need To Get Rid of the Sarcasm.

Our children are depending on us to teach them about life. They're surrounded by friends all day. The last thing that they need when they get home is another friend. We need to meet them as their parent. As a parent who loves them, more than a person who likes them or worse, wants to be liked by them. When my step on me children first came into my life, a couple of them said that they really liked me and blah, blah, blah. I'm sure you get the picture. My response was something to the effect of "We'll see if that's true when you're fourteen." That may have seemed like a mean thing to say, but I understood the reality of people—when they turn about fourteen, their bodies are flooded with hormones. They're gaining physical strength faster than any other time in their life, and all their friends have cell phones, etc. I really didn't have a grip on how much distain I would develop against them, though. This is where this transformation of "how I love them" changed me.

You're probably thinking, "I think, we read about something like this earlier." I agree, I think, you did too. A nod from the editor makes it conclusive. Here's the question, after being bombarded with the thousandth time of trying to educate this young, going-into-adulthood-soon person on why to shut the damn light off when they leave their room, once again. I have to ask: What's my delivery? I actually assessed this in my own life. I found I was slapping them with sarcasm that cut to the core and stated you're stupe. More importantly, love wasn't in the midst of the statements. There wasn't caring in the midst of it. As I listened to my family interact with each other I heard my replies of sarcasm as their answers in the midst of their conversations. Then I would tell them that's not the way to act toward each other . . . sarcastically of coarse. Shame on me and what I had modeled.

Although, on a positive note they are pretty good students.

Bottom line, does it really matter? I mean, ultimately, We learn what we learn by however that lesson was delivered to us. Does it really matter how we teach them? **Pick your battles** for sanity's sake, shut the light off yourself. Do the dishes yourself. Vacuum the house, guess what . . . self? You must never lose sight of the fact that you live in the house too, and you asked them into your life. Sometimes, it's better to stop pushing deeper into the wound in order to reaffirm the pain of remembrance of who's the adult, but show how important it is by doing the task at hand ourselves. The other side of this is of coarse to deal out consequences, but as stated before this a fine line of you verses them and the child producing parent that you bed with each night. The parent will usually go along with the consequence until they have to deal it out. Then guess who's trapped into doing the bastardly dastardly deed of enforcement . . . . verbal abuse anyone?

Back to love. Often with my son, I know he's an action away from doing something stupid for lack of a better word. Stupidity is defined as doing something you know that you shouldn't do, but you do it anyway. My daughter is about three minutes away from hitting that whining screech, that has broken windows, once her brother and she engaged in an activity. So half the time I'm loaded and ready to blow before I even start my interaction with them each day. As I turn the corner onto my street the thoughts of what hasn't gotten done today starts to surface.

Is this fair to me, to them, or the household? No!

The way to defuse the attitude of destruction is going to sound so nineties, but here goes. **Smile.**

When we've woke them up for school and they're coming down the hall with the dragging feet, smile. When I turn the corner on the street . . . Smile! This interaction of peace starts with love. Love is kind. Love is gentle. Love keeps no record of wrong doings. In other words, whatever requires grace is love. I'm not talking about giddy infatuation. I'm talking about it's time to set me aside and put others first, sacrifice.

Expect the answers that you're going to get when you say good morning. Be the adult and grow up the hell up!

Most of the battles, if any, that we have with our children are as if we have this need to convince them of our point. News flash! It's your dang! House!

You're the adult. You pay the bills! *Ding Ding*! Grow up! That eighties/sixties crap about our children being an adult trapped in a child's body has been disproved.

If by chance your teen is truly struggling in this transisiton from child to adolescense here's a big challenge if you want to see a big change, start out by doing some home schooling. Now, is this a guaranteed approach to reducing stress no, but it's an option. Sometimes the transition to middle school or high school is overwhelming due to the craziness that they're already dealing within their home. Often after about a year of home school and reduced interaction with current friends at school they'll realize that a change in attitude toward school and life in general may be worth it, for them. All I can attest to is it helped us. The deal for us was our child had to bring up and maintain their grades for a certain amount of time then we'd talk about going back to school. The biggest challenge is all individuals in humanity have a need to fit someplace, a need to have their spot, to deal with their dilemmas which can cause us to do stupid things.

I'm sure that even you have at least one stupid moment with a lack of maturity to reflect on in life.

Remember . . . . grace . . . . No not after school gym bleachers Grace . . . grace that tells our children I get it, I've been where your at. I just want to help you even though it will cost me. You are worth it. Action and time. Action and time. Words unspoken, yet, wisdom passed on.

# Coach's Perspective

When you were in school, did you love your teachers at all times? No. Did you love your coach at all times? No. Did you love your grandparents at all times? No. Why do you think that was?

It's because their job wasn't to be liked by you but to link you to a winning concept or idea that you hadn't thought of in your short span of life experiences. Coach's views are not to look at the size of the mountain that is before you their pupil but to focus on your strengths and what it takes to overcome the task at hand. They are hired and to be used as an organic plethora of experiences to help you attain victory in the situation that you are going into. Giving the emotions of whether you loved, hated, or liked them wasn't demanded by them, but respect was demanded. Often, respect was given as a gracious response to them. You would follow their advice unquestionably. Reason being, their motives were sensed without being said. They were more often concerned with what you needed in life at that moment more so than worrying about what you wanted. The price they were willing to pay was at your cost, not theirs.

All of the aforementioned demands of a coach do have a place in all of our abilities to grow. It's only our pride that could distance us from their immeasurable input, and they would respect our wishes gladly, then simply fade away.

Herein lies the truth, Mom or Dad can't, and usually won't, just let you go, and as children, we inherently know it. The lip comes out. The silence starts. The lack of eye contact starts, etc.

Listen, please, as parents leading tomorrow's generation, the rolling of the eyes or a silent moment is a small price to pay for the torture you're setting yourself up for, if you give in to letting them bully their way into being. I guarantee this, when you stand firm in your actions, you build a firm foundation for your children to build their lives on.

Lastly, as children, they don't get or understand our adult drive or craving to be married, and as youths, they simply don't care nor should they have to. In their lives, marriage has seemed to bring more chaos than clarity, and they do have a point by what they've experienced.

# Boys to Men

There actually was a time that people who were bad were identified by some of their behaviors and dress that differentiated them from people who were viewed as good folks for the lack of a better word. These bad people had tattoos, cussed every other woed, hit women, fought men to settle problems, smoked pot, and engaged in other not-so-healthy styles of life.

Now much of what was seen twenty years ago as anti societal is now the norm. The problem with this is now there isn't a clear standard to measure our choices against in order to see if what's encountered in life is either good or bad for our life or society as a whole. So confusion is prevalent everywhere. Not to say that we need to pass judgment on the interactions or ink on someone's body, but certain stereotypes used to fit and used to help us to have a reasonable response to someone when we met them for the first time. How they speak, dress, and allow their bodies to look, spoke volumes about who they are, where, or what they may become. It was called a first impression, and it is not to be confused with judging the person.

Now as we venture out into the cosmetic culture of the bling, bling, and bling of today, we are introduced to image. Now, image is everything, fake it till you make it. Well, what happens if, as many people will attest to, you don't make it? In fact, the act of faking it has now made you nothing but a very good faker. You've now become the image. A great faker is all you are, you're empty and pretty useless as far as producing something positive for society. If you think this statement is pretty blatant, then simply tour your regional ghettos, . . . Thousands of minds being treated and allowed to live as less.

Don't misunderstand me, I'm not stating that the people who live in these areas are of no value, but the product of their lives is more a detriment than cement for the foundation of their and ultimately our society. Whatever the excuse is, it doesn't matter. Much of what they've come to represent is image and materialism. Izz gots to getz minezzez. What a mess that we've fostered and allowed to progress as we've elected our leaders, who do not seem to want to deal with our neighborhoods needs, but are quick to shove money to abortion clinics to remedy what abstinence could do taught by a parental figure of enforcement. All this is because we believe that "As long as I get mine, what does it matter who's affected? As our ghettos swell and our elderly becomes more dependant, who will step up to fill the void? You see, when we're all focused on "me," we forget about "we." The only difference between we and me is the letter "m" or "w." or better yet a," w" turned up side down. But the lives that we can have an affect on living through the commitment that the, "w," can bring is **ginormous!**

You may question: What does any of this waa . . . waa . . . opinionated rhetoric have to do with me anyhow? Exactly, that's the point exactly. The better question is, what is your motive toward this family being subjected to your life? Once you join their family, there is no more "me" . . . as you've hopefully come to know by now.

There is no more "me" as in mine. There is no more "me" as in material items rule. There is no more "me" as in my house, my car, my woman, my dog, my cat, my fish, my yard, my mom, my dad, my church, whatever. So how does someone change their focus and not remain in the maze of "me," "myself," and "I"?

The answer is actually as easy . . . time. If you don't have the time for the children involved because it's Friday night at the club, Saturday afternoon with my boys, it's Christmas with mommy, hey wake up!!!!! your taking on a family who will now depend on your descisions to make there life as you would have liked your own to be. You can have an affect in changing their lives from temper tantrums and turmoil, to happiness and stability.

Once again I'll state the bible will lead you where your life experiences may have failed you. Read the book of James. Perserverance, persistance, humility, patience, but don't expect to be a hero that's hollywood and herasy. Life is all you got and then some. With out this attitude our families, nieghborhoods, cities and states are lost. Democracy cannot thrive without integrity, honesty, and unity just look at the state of our nation today.

In conclusion, I hope I've pissed you off a little because pain causes passion and with that you'll either feed your self and you'll find the door, or you'll realize the opportunity you'll be embracing that will cost you your life. In order to become a part of this puzzle you'll need to be honest. Honesty demands us to look at ourselves and in this case of being stepped on, our true motives for connecting to this family has to be looked into.

As for myself and my wife we have been married for nine years. We've seen some of our own friends marry and divorce and marry again. Once again judging is not taking place here. I just notice the drive for people to be part of some thing bigger. The reasons why we marry doesn't matter as much as the fortitude to finish the race. I am not trying to paint a picture of bliss by any means for our marriage. In fact, most of the reason I wrote this book with a work book to follow is because of the turmoil and unforsen bull that I've faced. Confusion, betrayal, and abandonment on some level we're both guilty of. Yet with our motive being to focus on the children having a place to call home and a family to learn life skills from, we choose to persevere. As I truly conclude here . . . What type of morning would you have liked to wake up to as a child? What type of home work atmosphere would you have liked? Prayers with mom each night as you were tucked in or silence in order to sleep peacefully. Holidays despising parents or digesting food on your own couch? The answer to these questions can now be lived out in your home with your family. You're . . . . now . . . . the . . . . ADULT.

Made in the USA
Monee, IL
28 March 2021